MW00399288

Clockwork

Clockwork

Time-Saving Routines and Tested Strategies for Success

Michael S. Snell

ROWMAN & LITTLEFIELD
Lanham • Boulder • New York • London

Published by Rowman & Littlefield
A wholly owned subsidiary of The Rowman & Littlefield Publishing Group, Inc.
4501 Forbes Boulevard, Suite 200, Lanham, Maryland 20706
www.rowman.com

Unit A, Whitacre Mews, 26-34 Stannary Street, London SE11 4AB

Copyright © 2017 by Michael S. Snell

All rights reserved. No part of this book may be reproduced in any form or by any
electronic or mechanical means, including information storage and retrieval systems,
without written permission from the publisher, except by a reviewer who may quote
passages in a review.

British Library Cataloguing in Publication Information Available

Library of Congress Cataloging-in-Publication Data

Library of Congress Cataloging-in-Publication Data Available

ISBN 978-1-4758-2937-2 (cloth : alk. paper)
ISBN 978-1-4758-2938-9 (pbk. : alk. paper)
ISBN 978-1-4758-2939-6 (electronic)

∞ ™ The paper used in this publication meets the minimum requirements of American
National Standard for Information Sciences Permanence of Paper for Printed Library
Materials, ANSI/NISO Z39.48-1992.

Printed in the United States of America

To my wife Jill, the master of routines for our family and my best
friend—thank you for making our family run like clockwork
all these years.

To my children, Michael and Alexandra, who made me a father and who
make me prouder to be theirs with each passing day.

Contents

Contents

Preface

Did you have a favorite piece of playground equipment as a child? Was it a very large swing set? Or, perhaps, the monkey bars? (Both of these are basically outlawed today, by the way.) What about the merry-go-round? For some, the merry-go-round was a source of endless childhood joy; a place where children could spin endlessly, out of control, become dizzy and enjoy a great laugh. For others—those children susceptible to motion sickness—the merry-go-round was to be avoided. Far too often, there was one kid from the neighborhood who took too much joy in turning the merry-go-round faster and faster, ignoring the pleas of some unfortunate kid who did not enjoy the feeling of spinning endlessly, out of control.

Fast forward to adulthood. There is still a merry-go-round. You can find it in the office and at home. There are still "kids" (okay, now coworkers), who enjoy spinning your world and controlling your whirlwind. How much of the spin do you control? Is it healthy to believe that you can control some or all of the spin? Would you like to?

This book will help you control your merry-go-round. It will help you balance the spinning of your day, night, and life. Everyone falls prey to the spin; and the speed of the world is surely not slowing. We need to recognize the spin and implement a system of routines to manage it.

This book is for those who want to improve, whether you are a superintendent, assistant superintendent, CEO, principal, teacher, parent, or leader. Throughout the book, the title of superintendent is used. Feel free to insert your title and begin your journey. Also, the book mostly assumes you are using some type of technology to record appointments and tasks, and take notes. If this is not completely true in your circumstance, feel free to adapt the suggestions to your system. The routines mentioned in this book can and should be adapted and improved upon.

There are two memories from my childhood that led to an interest in organization. In elementary school, I remember being summoned to the teacher's desk. For what, I do not recall, but I do remember I was only slightly taller than her desk. The teacher opened her desk drawer—you know, the old-school teacher desk with four to six drawers that pull out the entire way. When the drawer opened, in front of me lay an organizational vista that I can recall today. She grabbed something for me and closed the drawer too soon for my gawking eyes, but the desk drawer was organized to the nines. From that day forward, I was hooked and could not wait to have my first, organized teacher's desk.

The other memory is from my father's office. It was in high school and, every once in a while, I picked him up from work (in those days, not every kid had a car). I was led into his office and sat in front of his desk, looking around in amazement at his organized workspace. As he packed up, he took everything off the worktable and every other surface, for that matter. So, as you can imagine, each day my office desk, table, and all surfaces are cleared of papers and projects.

It is funny how simple moments like these can lead to who you are and how you behave. These two moments led me toward a successful system to set up files, manage multiple priorities and millions of dollars, and also to be a better father, spouse, son, board member, community member, and leader.

ONE REQUEST

As you read about my system, please resist the urge to say, "I already do that." When you do, you disengage from any possibility of improvement. Organization is not rocket science. However, consistent attention and implementation of such a system often eludes us! There are still days and weeks where we all fail to execute at the levels we are capable, and times when we are stuck on the merry-go-round. Welcome to the human race and the spin. Refocus, recommit, and work your system.

Chances are, if you are reading this book, you recognize the need to be better organized. One piece of advice, regardless if you are a first time manager, teacher, principal, or superintendent—never arrive. Let me say it again—never arrive. Always improve. A job title or position should not interfere with constant growth. There is value in a journey to improve your routines. For some, it might be an evolution. For others, it might be a revolution.

ONE ACTIVITY

What's on your plate? What are your obligations and to whom? Professional? Personal? Find a blank paper plate and draw a line down the center. At the top of one half, write "personal" and write "professional" on the other. Spend a few minutes listing all your commitments. When finished, ask yourself the following about the commitments you listed:

- Are there too many?
- Are there too few?
- What commitments are of most value to you?
- What commitments are of least value to you?
- Are there commitments to eliminate?
- Are there commitments to add?

Everyone has a plate. The benefit of this exercise is to have you own *your* plate. Keep the plate handy as you read this book. It can serve as a healthy reminder of what is important to you, what is required of you, and how you plan to accomplish all of your hopes and dreams.

What if this system could save you an hour a day? Would you subscribe to it? What would you do with the bonus "me time"? More work or more family? After viewing your plate, where could that "me time" best be put to use? You have choices:

- You can invest in the paper plate activity or not.
- You can continue reading the book or not.
- You can commit to improving who you are or not.

You can commit to improving your management of everything so you can lead or not. Choose well.

Acknowledgments

Thank you to the team of people who helped throughout the process of writing this book:

Julie Randall Romig—for her assistance with copy editing and counsel.

Jill, Michael, and Alexandra Snell—for their feedback on the book and counsel.

Harry Snell—for being a great father and proofreader.

Sally Janora—for being a wonderful mother-in-law and proofreader.

Pat Crawford and Jim Buckheit—from the Pennsylvania Association for School Administrators for their support of the article that led to this book.

Introduction

This book began one summer as a hope and a dream for me while I conducted my yearly review (see chapter 13) at the beach. Organization, time management, task management, and managing twenty-four hours each day have and will always be of interest to me. I started by writing an article for superintendents about simple routines that help you succeed daily, weekly, monthly, and yearly; my hope and dream, and that article, resulted in what you are holding in your hands.

It is an honor to share my system and routines that have evolved along with me through my journey from teacher to assistant principal, principal, assistant superintendent, and now superintendent. These routines are practiced with a fabulous team in a wonderful school district that I am humbled to lead.

The book is organized into four areas for your consideration.

- Daily—The first section of this book reviews routines that you do daily. It begins with a process called the "Daily Setup" and continues to review daily meetings, files, schedules, tasks, note taking, and delegation.
- Weekly—The second section presents a weekly review that will enable you to reflect and project into the future regarding your calendar and tasks. It also covers weekly meetings and weekly tasks.
- Monthly—The third section covers monthly meetings and tasks. It also introduces a monthly "Leadership Lunch with Me" that helps you focus on who you are as a professional and who you are in your personal life.
- Yearly—The final chapter reviews the value of a year-end reflection and an opportunity to plan for the upcoming year.

Each section will provide routines to implement and adapt to your preferences as you proceed along your journey to becoming a more efficient and effective leader. You may read the book from front to back, or jump to a chapter that appeals to you right now. I would, however, suggest reading chapter 1 first, as it presents a routine that will become the foundation of each day.

Take one chapter, one routine, and get started. Feel comfortable to adapt the suggestion to what works for you and your current organizational level. Remember, change will not take place overnight. The goal is to improve the management of your day-to-day world that enables you to lead your family, your work, and your life.

At the end of each chapter, there is a bulleted list of action items under the heading "Let's Get Started." Add them to your task list and take one step at a time. One approach might be to read a chapter each week or month, and focus on implementing that chapter's action items. Consider how a colleague or a team might join in a book read and create some peer accountability throughout the process. Not only will you learn new tips from this book, but also from your colleagues through a collaborative dialogue.

Let's get started!

Part One

Daily Routines

In the first part of this book, we will focus on the routines that occur daily that, for the most part, you complete without even thinking about. Examples include your daily meetings, files and filing, your schedule, tasks and projects, delegation, and note taking. Taken as a whole, they consist of what you do on most days. As you read the first part, start to reflect on all the daily routines that begin when your alarm clock wakes you, until it is time to set it again and return to sleep. What do you do each day that could become routine? How can you "off-load" any number of decisions and activities so you can be fully present in your day job and for your family? The first chapter begins with the Daily Setup and provides the perfect routine, each day, to maximize the next twelve-plus hours that are in front of you.

Chapter One

The Daily Setup

Who you are is a by-product of the many microdecisions you make each day. Some of these decisions become so routine that you make them on autopilot, such as:

- What time to awaken;
- What to eat for breakfast;
- What to wear; and
- What route to use while traveling to work.

We are all creatures of habit and routine. Some enhance your productivity while others hinder you. What if there were routines to improve your control of your merry-go-round? What if a better command of your day improved your ability to be more fully present in conversations with others?

This chapter will provide you with a framework for creating a more deliberate and effective routine in your workplace, beginning with the first moments you spend in your office each morning.

ARRIVAL

What do you do following your arrival at the office? Are there many hellos and small conversations that lead to the loss of the first thirty minutes or more of your day? While that might happen on occasion, it should be the exception, not the rule. Adopting the Daily Setup will help avoid losing minutes each morning and hours each week.

The process for the Daily Setup consists of four components:

1. Check-In
2. Process in-basket and task list
3. Review tasks
4. Review schedule

Check-In

Almost every day begins with a "Hello" to an administrative assistant and a brief review of any pressing items that require your immediate attention. While checking in with your assistant, unpack your briefcase, set up your technology, and complete whatever brief activities you need to start your day (such as securing a cup of coffee). When you return to your office, part ways with your assistant and close your door.

This check-in process should take approximately five minutes. Conduct this activity each day, regardless of your arrival time. For example, there may be an early community board meeting downtown that delays arrival to the office until later in the day. Conduct your Daily Setup on arrival at your office.

Process In-Basket and Task List from Yesterday

The in-basket, and there should be only one in an office, is the next stop in your Daily Setup. Remove all contents from your in-basket and place them in the center of your workspace. These could be loose items that you have yet to file, items placed in the basket as you left the office the day before, or any items your assistant has placed there. Take a moment to review each item and ask yourself: What is the next action required? Most often, you will either handle each item quickly, or file for future reference (more detail on filing will be provided in chapter 3). Your in-basket review is also an opportunity to record any ideas or tasks that are on your mind. Add these items to your existing task list from the previous day and note any projects or tasks that are occupying your mind.

Your daily printed calendar with your daily task list is next for you to review (this is presented in chapter 4). Quickly scan for any handwritten notes or tasks from yesterday and record these as new tasks in your system. Also review the items from yesterday that you did not complete, as well as any notes you may have written underneath your appointments.

The goal of processing your in-basket and prior day's task list is to address any loose items, whether physical or mental, and complete them quickly or file them for future completion. If you follow this process first thing every day, your in-basket should remain relatively empty and piles will not form around your office. The goal is to return your in-basket to zero every day and not use it as a filing location.

Review Tasks

When you receive a request for assistance or are assigned a task, it is critical that you record the request immediately in writing or in task management software that you can view electronically and carry with you throughout your day. How many tasks, or "to-dos," do you record on your daily list? How many do you actually complete each day? What must you complete today and what items are tasks that will advance the completion of a larger project or goal?

When reviewing your tasks, the first step is to be honest with yourself and determine how many items you might complete today and how many items can be pushed into the future. Review all tasks on your list and choose ten of the most important or time-sensitive. This requires you to prioritize various tasks competing for your time and attention.

Using the "push factor" is one way to determine which ten tasks remain on today's list. The "push factor" is the number of days you can delay the task while still finishing it in a timely fashion or by an established deadline.

There are several types of pushes:

- Push to tomorrow—If you have a task that cannot be completed today, and is not due today, push this task to tomorrow by assigning it for review the next day.
- Push to a future date—This requires knowledge of deadlines and commitments to others. Is this task part of a larger team project? Are you waiting for someone else's action to move forward? If the project is due in three weeks, you might push it out for a week. Ultimately, your current workload and requirements will dictate the length of the push.
- Push to Saturday—When a task idea surfaces, it needs to be recorded in a paper calendar or in task management software. Very often, they are ideas or thoughts that are not critical to schedule at this time. So, list it and push to the next Saturday. This enables at least a weekly review of items that are not critical. Reviewing "Saturday" tasks can take place on the weekend or during your Daily Setup on Monday morning. If it is still just an idea that you don't want to lose, push to the next Saturday, or several Saturdays from this week. This will keep the idea alive until you decide it is actionable or no longer valid, at which point you will simply delete it. The key is to develop a system to record and remind you of tasks and ideas whenever you decide.

The goal of reviewing tasks daily is to create a plan of action that can survive its collision with reality. If you find a few unexpected minutes in your day, this daily processing and prioritizing will provide a quick answer as to what to do next.

Review Schedule

After you review your in-basket and tasks, the next step is to review your daily schedule. You can review scheduled appointments for the day, as well as look for opportunities to schedule quiet time to complete your ten tasks. Keep the following in mind as you review your schedule: Do you have the necessary files or documentation for your meetings today? Have you completed necessary tasks for your meetings today?

The open spaces in your calendar are opportunities to schedule your most pressing tasks for the day. In fact, you may want to make an appointment with a task, and yourself, for one hour and treat it like any other meeting. If the task is part of a project, schedule other appointments with this task in the coming days and weeks.

Taking time to review all that is required of you, including tasks and appointments, on a daily basis, is a habit that will save you time each day. The habit also creates a daily sense of balance when an idea, issue, or potential crisis emerges. You know your schedule and the tasks that require your immediate attention and action. Now you can determine where the emerging issue fits into your day.

There are several options when this occurs where you might:

- Determine that the issue is not pressing and ignore;
- Delegate the issue to someone else;
- Record the issue for future prioritizing and follow-up;
- Decide the issue needs immediate attention from others and call a quick meeting or make a phone call; or
- Decide the issue needs your immediate action and respond accordingly.

OPEN THE DOOR TO YOUR DAY

The final part of your Daily Setup is to open the door and say hello to your day. Now that you have a prioritized plan for the day, you should meet again with your assistant. Review your schedule and tasks and secure any files or other items from your assistant that you will need to complete your work. This brief follow-up meeting with your assistant is an opportunity for any of the following activities:

- Examine your schedule and discuss meetings, locations, travel times, or other support he or she can provide for each meeting;
- Discuss attendees for each meeting and how they should be greeted and brought into the meeting space;
- Review the most pressing tasks on your list and discuss how your assistant may provide support; and

- Identify any "open loop" items requiring follow-up, such as phone calls and e-mails that are awaiting a response.

We all hear the excuse that "I don't have time" to do this or that. Everyone fights the same battles of control, people, and deadlines. Those who renew and prioritize each day will find more clarity than those who do not. By implementing a Daily Setup, you are creating a routine that will prepare you to successfully complete your work each day.

One final note—the following chapters will address several items related to the Daily Setup and provide more direction on how to adapt and tailor these items to suit your needs. As you read more about creating and tracking tasks and managing your schedule, the Daily Setup will make even more sense. Take one step at a time and make one change at a time. Begin to reflect on the actions you already take and ask yourself—is there a better way?

LET'S GET STARTED!

- Review your daily schedule and make time for the first twenty to thirty minutes of your day.
- Communicate with your assistant regarding this new routine and your expectations.
- Communicate with your team and explain why your door will be shut for the first twenty to thirty minutes of the day.
- Create one in-basket and one out-basket.
- Keep reading for additional clarification on tasks, files, and the calendar.

Chapter Two

Daily Meetings

Meetings are a way of life for those in leadership and management roles. If you lead and are responsible for organizing and facilitating meetings, then meetings are what you do. However, most meetings should be a planned part of the week and not appear out of thin air.

How much time do you spend in any kind of meeting a day, week, or month? One key metric for you to calculate is your salary converted to an hourly wage. In other words, "What is your time worth per hour?" A simple calculation will determine this:

Yearly Salary	$100,000
Divided by	÷
	2,080 hours
	$48/hour

There are 2,080 total hours in a full-time, forty-hour workweek each year. This is a base calculation, as many leaders work well beyond forty hours each week. However, it is a critical calculation. Do you know how much the last one-hour meeting you attended cost your company? How about the cost to your company for the last hour you spent looking for a file, entertaining two colleagues that walked by, taking a mini-vacation on the Internet or fielding an unplanned phone call?

Now that you know your hourly rate, what value do you place on your time? If meetings are what you do, how valuable are they to the organization? How valuable are they to you and your goals? Track your activity today or review your activity from yesterday, and ask yourself if you are using your time wisely. Are you conducting the activities that are essential for the organization and commensurate with your salary?

In future chapters, the concept of routine meetings, whether weekly or monthly, will be presented. These are the meetings that should appear in your daily schedule and become the typical flow of your day. There are also other meetings that are scheduled by either you or your assistant from time to time. The rest of this chapter will alert you to other types of meetings that occur, advice on working with your assistant, phone calls, your door, and break time.

POP-UP MEETINGS

Pop-up meetings are all the conversations, phone calls, or interruptions that take place in between your scheduled appointments. You will also find these on the way to the restroom, break room, when you venture to your mailbox, and when you enter or exit the building. How many times are you amazed at what time you *actually* enter your car compared to what time you left your office? One or two conversations and the next thing you know, you are in the middle of a pop-up meeting. Keep daily meetings that are unplanned and unannounced to a minimum.

Certainly, emergencies and other issues arise that need immediate attention. As you read additional chapters, keep in mind your hourly rate and the need for you to control the cadence of meetings and other items that demand your attention.

EMERGENCIES

Emergencies happen. Try as you might, things occur that require your immediate attention. However, your Daily Setup should make clear whether the emergency warrants an interruption to your previously scheduled activities. Here are some examples of types of "emergencies" for your frame of reference:

- Safety—When there is a safety risk, it requires immediate action. There are times when you may be pulled from your work or meeting to respond to a serious concern for health or safety. No question, you must attend to these.
- "Emergency"—There are times when others consider what is before them at that moment to be an emergency. You must first determine if it really is a crisis and then decide if the crisis requires your attention. This is a critical question to ask. If you create a work culture that requires your attention to everything, then everything will come your way. Your office staff and team members will always interrupt you because you are the

answer or have the solution. If you determine it is not a crisis, refer the "emergency" back to its owner.

- Someone's Failure to Plan—A colleague comes barreling into your office with an urgent request and deadline and needs your assistance. This will happen, and you need to determine your involvement. When do you assist and when do you refer the issue back to the person? In your role as superintendent, you can delegate everything but final responsibility. Even though you are not responsible for the current situation, you are ultimately responsible for everything. This might be a learning opportunity for your team member, as well as for you.

EXECUTIVE ASSISTANT

Having an assistant is a wonderful gift. When you consider that you spend as much time, if not more, with your assistant each day than your family, the relationship is paramount to your success. One piece of advice: refer to the individual as an executive assistant. As a superintendent, you are the executive of an organization. It not only validates your job, but his or her job as well. A successful relationship with your executive assistant can elevate you and your career.

The Daily Setup begins with a conversation with your assistant upon your arrival. You rely on your assistant to provide you with "environmental scans" (phone calls, e-mails, mail or other matters) throughout the day. Following your Daily Setup, have another conversation with your assistant. There are days that meetings seem to pile up, which create brief moments to have conversations with your assistant throughout the day.

What is your routine at the end of the day? Better yet, what is your routine at the end of your assistant's day? Here is another opportunity for a brief conversation to close out the day. The point is that, throughout your day, you will have many conversations with your assistant, regardless of the length or if they require a sit-down meeting. Manage this relationship, one conversation at a time, and extend the utmost respect for what your assistant does for you and the organization.

One final piece of advice: If possible, plan to arrive to work after your assistant's arrival. The early morning is probably the part of the day that you control the most. Exercise, read, write, and eat a healthy breakfast. Arriving thirty minutes after your assistant enables that person to prepare for your arrival. Immediately following your good morning greetings, your assistant can provide you with items that need your attention. While this may not fit your situation, there are ways to have similar conversations to start the day.

Chapter 2

YOUR DOOR

What does an open door policy mean? If you are the leader or boss, what do you think it means? What would members on your team say? Another equally important question to ask is this: Can a passerby look into your office and see if you are there? Here is another conversation to have with your assistant, who is ultimately responsible for the traffic flow in and out of your office. There are times to have an open door policy. There are times to be seen and walk slowly through the hallways and even take a break. These times should be orchestrated and part of the schedule and flow of your day. There are other times to close the door and have a meeting with yourself. There are times to close the door and work on one big important project. It is okay to close your door from time to time and think. Go ahead and try it now.

Determine when to close your door and communicate this to your assistant and team. It is important for you to model this practice and expect it from others on your team. Have the conversation with your team and let them know it is acceptable to close their doors from time to time to complete work. What is the routine for someone to access you when your door is closed? This is another conversation for you to have with your assistant.

It is important for you to complete a majority of your work during the workday. The opposite of this is to always have an open door policy, accomplish little during the day, and take work home at night and on the weekends. If you are the superintendent, what you do sends messages throughout the organization. While we all have to take work home from time to time, this is not a long-term strategy for a balanced life. Model the need to close your door at times to complete work and make sure others do the same. Your subordinates want to succeed at work and at home, too.

DAILY PHONE CALLS

A phone call is a meeting. How many phone calls do you receive a day? Whether you admit it or not, most phone calls are unscheduled meetings that will take time from your day. Please have a conversation with your assistant about when to be interrupted by a phone call. Not all calls are of equal importance. Here is some advice:

- Never take an unsolicited sales call. The standard reply is that you are in a meeting and your assistant will take a message.
- Rarely take an unscheduled phone call. Your assistant can take a message and you can prioritize the appropriate time to respond.

- Determine a list of people who may have access to you whenever they call. This should be family and team members. This is another critical conversation to have with your assistant.
- Never answer your own phone unless you have caller ID and know the caller. Your family and other important people will have access to your cell phone and can reach you there.
- Allow your assistant to hold your cell phone while in meetings. Provide direction when to answer calls on your cell phone. Consider it an extension of any other phone and allow him or her to screen calls here as well.

When you arrive back in your office, you should review any phone calls that have come in and prioritize them with your assistant. This will also allow you to determine when to return phone calls. One option is to schedule time each day to return calls in batches. There might be opportunities throughout your day in between meetings to return calls. Consider travel time as a good time to return calls.

BREAK TIME

There are only so many hours in a day and there is only one you. If you rarely take time for lunch, you need to do so every once in a while. Treat yourself! Many executives will eat a sandwich or snack at their desk. While there is nothing wrong with this, there are also times to get up and move about. If you wear a device that counts steps, a desk job can be a killer when it comes to setting goals for movement throughout your day. Consider times throughout your day where you plan a "walk-about," or a quick trip to the back of the office just for the movement. It will clear your head and get the blood flowing through your body. It is also an opportunity for others to talk with you for a moment and reduces the need to disrupt you later in the office.

Your day is largely what you, not others, make it. As you read additional chapters, you will learn how planning weekly and monthly meetings will populate your days. There should be a cadence to your week as much as possible. Meetings are what we do. Weekly meetings with direct reports and monthly meetings with your team will help you stay connected to the organization and everything for which you are, ultimately, responsible.

LET'S GET STARTED!

- Calculate your hourly wage rate.
- Review the last few days and identify various types of pop-up meetings.
- Have a conversation with your assistant regarding:

- Your door;
- Phone calls; and
- Emergencies.

Chapter Three

Files

What is the first thing you notice when you walk into someone's office? The amount of papers and files lying around? Their workspace—clean or cluttered? Despite the growth in electronic documents and the decline in printed materials, most offices and professionals still interact with a mix of files within their workspaces. Creating a system that streamlines your filing practices and ensures you have information easily available to you, regardless of where it is stored, is critical to your success.

Consider your own office. You should view your office chair as the center of a military tank. The turret on a tank is the rotating weapon platform that can turn 360 degrees. Are you able to turn in your office chair and access many of the items you need? Take this little test—sit in your office chair and determine how many of the items you need are within your reach while seated. For example, can you quickly reach your stapler, paper clips, notepads, aspirin, calculator, and highlighters?

You should treat your files the same way, keeping the ones you need often within reach. Take the same test, above, but with your files. Can you reach your files from your chair? Must you stand and take a few steps or walk outside your office? Could you quickly grab what you need for upcoming meetings and current pressing issues?

Next, consider how you will organize your files to increase productivity and limit interruptions to your workflow. What do you do with the piece of paper in your hand right now? Where can you file it to minimize the stack and shuffle of papers? Your in-basket can serve as the starting point for successful file organization or it can serve as a repository where incoming items accumulate at an alarming and overwhelming rate.

The system detailed throughout the rest of this chapter will focus on access, retrieval, storage, and placement of filed items. Again, consider what you currently do or have and what possibilities might exist to improve upon your system and ultimately increase your efficiency and effectiveness at work.

MASTER FILES

Everyone needs one location in which to store his or her master files. The location will be determined by you and by your office layout. Master files are arranged alphabetically and should be labeled by subject in a manner that enables easy recall and makes sense to you. The decision to use manila or hanging folders, again, is one of personal preference. Bottom line: you need one file cabinet or location that holds your master files.

The location of master files depends on how many you have and how often you need the contents of these files. Ideally, your master files should be easily accessible from your chair or desk. If you have a small number of master files, you may be able to gather and interact with them on your own. As your master files grow, you may need another location in which to store them; in this case, your assistant may maintain and manage master files within his or her office.

HOT FILES

If your master files are located out of reach or outside of your office, set up a file drawer in your office referred to as "hot files." These files are needed routinely, for a specific time period, or for a temporary subject. For example, hot files may be used:

- To store monthly meeting materials, such as ideas for discussion, articles to review, and sample agendas for upcoming meetings;
- For timely projects that will require one-to-two months of work before returning them to your master files; and
- To house materials related to pressing or recurring issues requiring your daily or weekly attention.

ALPHA FILES

This idea is a revolutionary one that will remove single sheets of paper from your workspace. Select a file drawer within easy reach and do the following:

- Gather thirty-one hanging file folders:
- Label a hanging folder for every letter of the alphabet (A, B, C . . . Z) and then create five more with labels 1, 2, 3, 4, 5; and

- Hang them in a file drawer within easy reach and begin with the process outlined below.

As you review each piece of paper currently on your desk, or as materials accumulate in your in-basket, ask yourself this question: "What is expected of me?" If the task can be done in short order, do it. If not, it must be filed for future reference and completion.

Let's run through an example. Say you receive a hard copy of an agenda for a meeting next week. If there is a master file nearby, it might be one solution to ensure the paper does not end up on your desk or tabletop. Another option is to file it in your Alpha File for future recall. If the agenda is for a leadership team meeting, you have to determine the appropriate letter file that makes sense to you. In this case, file it in "L" and follow a simple rule.

The rule is this—as soon as you place the agenda in Alpha File "L," immediately record it in the title of the appointment. This will do two things: remove paper from your desktop or in-basket and create a location from which you can retrieve the information when needed. Here is the example mentioned with the title of the meeting and location:

- Leadership Team Meeting AFL

When you arrive at work on the day of the meeting and review your appointments, the "AFL" notation will remind you that you stored the agenda in your "L" Alpha File. You can quickly open your drawer and find the "L" file and retrieve your agenda. Consider how this can include other materials for future meetings that will no longer end up on top of your desk.

Let's try another example with a task. Today, you find a three-page state report that requires you to prepare comments and share with others. It is a task with a deadline and requires more than one minute of your time. Again, if there is a master file nearby, that may be the appropriate location for the report until you organize time to complete it. You can also make it a hot file. If neither choice will work for you, determine the letter of the alphabet under which to categorize it and add it to your To-Do List. An example of the name could be:

- Review State Report AFS

When you determine the task needs to be completed, you will be reminded that you temporarily filed it in your Alpha File letter "S." Again, you may have recorded this task and scheduled it for a week later because the deadline is really two weeks away. This is part of your Daily Setup mentioned in chapter 1. Chapter 5 will present the recording and labeling of tasks in more detail.

Your Alpha File is also convenient for storing items that do not require a permanent file. You might have a few favorite restaurant menus and you know they are located in "AFR." There might be conference opportunities that you place in "AFC" or vacation materials that are placed in "AFV."

You may be wondering what about the files labeled 1–5? These are filing spaces for you to place items that need a home and make sense to your office. For example, file "#1" could hold all contact directories and file #2 could hold all employee contracts. When you need to make contact with a colleague or someone at a state agency or organization, you know the directories are in file "#1." Other items for numbered files may include blank tablets and meeting note forms (see chapter 6 for an explanation and example of a meeting note form). Review the papers and files that currently reside on the top of your workspace and consider the possibilities. You may need more than five numbered files.

Implementing an Alpha File system will assist you with the papers you currently find visible in and around your office. The key is to remember to record each item placed in an Alpha File as a task or appointment if applicable. This will help you easily retrieve items contained in these files when needed.

Finally, create a routine to review all files and purge items that are no longer of value. Often, you will place items here and discover it is time to discard them within a few months of filing. This will keep your Alpha Files relatively thin and easily manageable. See chapter 5 for an explanation of this task.

PROJECT FILES

What projects are on your plate right now? What filing space do you have in your office to hold these major project files? Some example projects may include developing your organization's budget, creating a strategic plan, a real estate transaction, or policy review. The size may vary, but there are usually multiple files related to these major projects, and you will need to locate them in one central area.

Consider using a single file drawer if you have the space for each project, or use a lateral file and break the drawer into several parts for each project. Ideally, these should be located as close to your chair as possible to allow for easy access.

The budget process is a good example of a file drawer that holds last year's, this year's, and next year's budgets as the project moves forward. Review these locations with your assistant so he or she knows what project drawers you create. This will eliminate the need to have these and other files sitting on top of tables and desks and provide for quick access. It also provides a place to return all files at the close of the day or work session.

TICKLER FILE

The tickler file is another filing option and is quite simple. There are times when a hot file or an Alpha File will do just fine for the piece of paper in your hand. However, there are times when you want to be reminded of something on a certain date. The tickler file is the place to locate physical items, cards, or objects for later retrieval and requires daily attention from either you or your assistant.

Here is how to get started:

- Purchase forty-three manila file folders;
- Label thirty-one files with a single number on each (1, 2, 3, etc.) to represent each day of the month; and
- Label twelve files with a single month on each (January, February, March, etc.).

Next, determine the location. If you will be monitoring the file daily, place these files in a drawer that can be reached from your office chair and checked each day. If your assistant will handle, he or she will need to locate the file for easy access daily.

Each day of the month, check the corresponding file each morning, or perhaps the next day's file before leaving each night. Let's say it is March 15, and you open the file and find a note you scratched out a few months ago to remind you it is a friend's birthday. Your tickler file will remind you of this on March 15, and you will be able to wish your friend "Happy Birthday." Some other examples include:

- A yearly reminder to purchase additional note cards for your office;
- A letter of concern or appreciation that you want to follow up on in two weeks;
- Birthday cards for significant others that are pre-purchased and placed ten days prior to each birthday; and
- An anniversary card—Enough said!

The remaining monthly files are usually kept behind the numbered files and accessed on the last day of the current month or first day of the new one. For example, if it is March 31, you will want to access the file titled "April," pull out all items, and refile them in the appropriate day in April. If you need to file a card for three months in the future, find the month and place it there until the last day of the previous month.

COMPUTER FILES

Have you ever peeked at someone's laptop and scanned what his or her desktop looks like? Do you have difficulty finding files on your computer, laptop, or tablet? Many of the same principles used to create an effective paper-based filing system hold true for electronic files. As more items are created and converted to electronic files, it is important to have a system here as well.

HARD DRIVE AND CLOUD FILES

There is similarity between your hard drive and cloud drive files and your master files. These files are arranged alphabetically and should be labeled by subject in a manner that enables easy recall. Create a folder and name it in a way that is relevant to you. Examples might include: Audits, Communications, Enrollment, Meetings, and Personnel. Keep the titles general and use as few words as necessary.

Due to the cyclical nature of most tasks, it is important to use subfolders within each general folder. For example, a file might have a general title of "Personnel" and then have several subfolders labeled for each year. Inside each year's folder, create additional folders with personnel matters from that year. Each year, you may need to provide a speech at graduation. Consider a file labeled "Speeches" and subfolders listing the event: "Graduation." Inside each of these subfolders, you would place folders labeled for each year you gave the speech (Graduation—2013, Graduation—2014, Graduation—2015).

This provides years of documentation to review speeches, files, and other materials. This system will also save time when you need to create agendas for recurring meetings. Simply open last year's retreat agenda or last month's meeting agenda and update it as needed. When completed, use the "Save As" feature and update with a new file name.

DESKTOP FILES

How many files can you place on the desktop of a laptop and still manage to find everything? There are those who push the limit and those who believe that placing a file on the desktop is akin to leaving clothing all over the floor of their bedroom rather than hanging it in the closet. The desktop can be a place of strategic value and a few simple tricks can keep it in that way.

The desktop should not be used as a storage place for all files. The desktop is not the place to save files for someday when you figure where they should really reside. No different from an in-box, as presented later in this chapter, you should not operate from this location.

If you find yourself in this position, dedicate some time to review each file and place it in your newly created master file on your hard drive. Another trick that will help is to ask yourself if you really even need to store a file. If you are sure, file. If you are unsure, create a folder on your desktop labeled "Desktop Files." Place items in here and wait thirty days. Place a reminder in your task list to "Review Desktop Folder Files" and schedule it to appear in thirty days. When review day arrives, you may be surprised to find that these all-important files are really not that important.

Another trick is to locate shortcuts or aliases on your desktop for recurring file access. One example is a meeting template to create a draft agenda for a meeting. Simply click the shortcut and begin to create the agenda. When changes are made to the template, use the "Save As" feature to save the file to the appropriate location in your master files on your hard drive. Other shortcuts and aliases might be an employee phone directory, board member committee assignments, and documents you might need in the middle of a meeting or when speaking with the press.

DAILY FILE FOLDERS

Every day, there are incoming items for your consideration and action such as signatures on numerous forms. Here is a simple method to differentiate each file's purpose by color. Consider using file folders made of light plastic that hold up well over time and stand out from other items placed in your in-basket.

- Signature File Folder (yellow)

  There are forms that require your signature, whether for use of vacation time or approvals for courses as per a collective bargaining agreement. While many such routine items are now electronic, they still require daily attention. If there are certain offices that require your signature, you may want to use a different color for each office (business office, special education office).

- Mail File Folder (purple)

  Any number of items is appropriate here, such as letters, magazines and journals, cards, and other business correspondence. A time-saving tip here is to have your assistant screen each item that contains a request and highlight the "ask" or the area of follow up required of you.

Consider other routine matters that require your attention and create a color-coded file folder. Working closely with your assistant, determine the color and frequency with which these items appear in your in-basket. For example, do you want to see routine mail each day? How might you save some time here and only see this file folder every couple of days? This would require a conversation and a shared understanding with your assistant as to when correspondence should be brought to your attention.

IN-BASKET AND OUT-BASKET

While many of the suggestions in this chapter centered on files, it is important to pay attention to your in-basket. The in-basket is the one location where items enter your office for action. The goal each day is to return your in-basket to "zero." It is not meant to be a filing solution for items that have yet to find a home. While it is a challenge on some days, work your system to keep paper and files here to a minimum, if not zero.

There are times at the end of the day to place a few loose items in your in-basket as you depart for home. If you conduct a Daily Setup each day, as mentioned in chapter 1, you will review these few items each day and file appropriately.

Your out-basket is the one location to place items for your assistant. Have a conversation with him or her to determine the frequency in which to enter your office to collect items. When you are finished with the signature folder, completed work with a file, or need some papers filed, place them here for your assistant.

The goal of this chapter, and your subsequent action, is to remove many of the papers and files that are often located on top of your desk and other workspace. Create filing locations mentioned here or adapt them to your personal situation. Next, gather all the papers and files in your office into one stack and begin.

LET'S GET STARTED!

- Have a conversation with your assistant regarding files in your office.
- Review and update your master files.
- Create a hot file.
- Create an Alpha File.

- Create a tickler file.
- Create project files and drawers for projects.
- Review and clean up your computer files.

Chapter Four

Schedule

We all have twenty-four hours or 1,440 minutes to manage each day. How do you use that time to work, play, sleep, and be present with family or friends? Examining your schedule can provide many clues to your struggle and success with time management. Reflecting on how you want to spend your time, compared to how you are actually spending your time, is the first step. This chapter will provide you with tips for determining how to use your time and practical advice for your schedule.

AUDIT YOUR TIME

Let's begin your time management reflection by asking yourself a few focusing questions: "During a normal day, when do I find my 'zone' at work?" "When do I feel burned out and in need of a break?" These and other questions offer insight into your work habits that will enable you to effectively schedule your day and maximize your productivity. For some, the early morning hours are the best time to focus on major projects; others are "in the zone" in the afternoon. The key is to find the best time of day for you to be in your "zone" and use this time for important projects or tasks.

Next, reflect over the last several weeks and take a look at your calendar. What do you see and notice? Are you using your zone times of the day for the most productive work? Now look out over the next two weeks and make necessary changes to use your time more effectively.

Here is an assignment for you over the next several weeks—conduct a time audit using a time utilization log. You can search online for numerous approaches and forms that fit your situation. Record your activities each hour using a countdown timer. Record your energy as high, medium, or low and other comments that might help in your review. At the end of two weeks,

look back and audit your use of time and determine your most productive
times of the day. You might consider completing this activity with your
assistant and engaging in a conversation with him or her at the end of your
audit. Use insight gained from the experience to adjust your calendar going
forward.

MANAGE YOUR SCHEDULE

Who "owns" the responsibility for your schedule? Who manages your schedule? You? Your assistant? Ultimately, you need to take responsibility for
your schedule—no one else. With only so many hours in the workday, the
sooner you take responsibility for your schedule, the better. The first step in
managing your schedule is to make time for your Daily Setup (chapter 1).
This simple routine will save you time with a prioritized daily plan of action
each day.

Next, make decisions about your time and communicate these decisions
to your team members. Your assistant can play a major role in managing
your schedule. After reading this chapter, sit with him or her and discuss
your schedule together. Consider the current state of doing business and
whether it is working for you. Do you want to improve finishing projects by
deadlines? Would you like to be home in time for your child's evening
activities more often? As you begin to make changes to your schedule, continue communicating with your assistant and relevant team members who are
impacted by your schedule and your availability.

Once you have determined how and why you want to manage your schedule a certain way, it's time to make time management hopes a reality. Begin
by determining who can place an event on your calendar. If you are the only
person who can do so, you will need to build time in your daily schedule for
ongoing interruptions to your work, including the following:

• Taking phone calls to review calendars with colleagues to select meeting
  dates;
• Reading and responding to e-mails to arrange meetings with you; and
• Receiving office visitors who want to schedule future meeting dates, and
  anything else that might come up.

Now think about how much time you will spend handling these interruptions and requests. What if you shifted this control of your calendar to your
assistant and empowered him or her to manage your calendar within parame-
ters you established? Some ideas:

- Do not schedule meetings from 8:00 to 8:30 a.m., the time for my Daily Setup;
- Schedule interviews only in the morning (or afternoon, depending on your preference); and
- Use thirty minutes as the default time for most appointments.

One final question about using your assistant to manage your schedule for any readers reluctant to try: if you review your hourly rate, is it the best use of your time to stop working and schedule each appointment? No. Remember, having an assistant is a gift. If you are fortunate to have one, use him or her to maximize your organization and productivity.

CHOOSE A CALENDAR

There is an ongoing debate about the type or style of calendar to use. What began as a paper-based business has evolved into a technological, app-driven world. The perfect system for you is the one that works, feels right, and allows you to access your information when necessary. Many professionals use Day-Timer, Franklin Covey, or Week-at-a-Glance paper-based tools. Some are sleek and can fit into a coat pocket. Others are wire-bound with sections for appointments, tasks, notes, and zippered pouches.

Technology provides a different type of portability as well as the ability to synchronize your calendar across multiple devices. It also enables your assistant to remotely access your calendar, tasks, and e-mail for further functionality. There are ways for team members to share calendars and request appointments within systems such as Outlook or GroupWise. When presented with the idea of an assistant accessing all of this information, some professionals cringe, while others see possibilities.

Ultimately your solution must work for you. Chances are you will tweak the ideas in this book and improve upon them for your particular circumstances. Share the ideas with others and see what evolves from a group conversation about organization. The following tips apply to a technological calendar solution. If you are happy with a paper-based solution, still consider how the overall concepts might translate to that format.

ENTERING APPOINTMENTS

Meetings comprise the vast majority of appointments on a leader's schedule. They are time-bound with a specific start and end time. The following tips will help in recording such appointments in your calendar:

- Meeting Title—Keep the title of the meeting to three words if possible. You need as little as possible to inform you of the meeting when it reappears in a few weeks. What abbreviations make sense for your meetings?
- Default Appointment Length—Set the default in your computer software program to the minimum time you will need. This might be thirty minutes or an hour, depending on your preferences. You can always edit this option if the first choice does not work best for you.
- Meeting Title and File Location—If you need a file for the meeting, list it in the title as mentioned in Chapter 3. If the location is in a HOT file, after the title, list "HOT." If the agenda is located in your Alpha File (AF), after the title list the location with the initial that corresponds to the topic or makes sense to you—AFW—Alpha File Washington. The meeting is with Mr. Washington, a community member.

  - Leadership Team Mtg – HOT: This title will tell you the meeting name and remind you to either take the entire file with you or look for material in that file to take along.
  - Nonprofit Board Mtg – AFW: This title tells you the nature of the meeting and that there is corresponding material in your Alpha File labeled "W."

- Meeting Location—Always list the location of your meetings. For offsite meetings, use the address to obtain directions by clicking on the link. In most phones, this will launch a GPS app for directions. For building locations that are in your organization, simply list the building name or room number.
- Alerts / Alarms—Based upon the travel time, consider setting a reminder that helps you depart for the meeting in a timely fashion. The alert time can be changed from minutes to hours. This is a conversation to have with your assistant as he/she enters appointments into your calendar.
- Categories—Some software enables you to list whether the appointment will display as busy, free, tentative, or out-of-the-office. Consider how these might inform you and others who have access to your calendar. There are times to consider this feature when teams share calendars and workspaces and times when it is not practical or warranted.
- Note Field—This is the most underused feature in an appointment window. Each time you enter information in the note field about an appointment, place an asterisk "*" at the end of the title. This indication reminds you that information is stored in the notes field. There might be additional directions for entering a building at an offsite meeting or parking information. You might want to copy a portion of an e-mail to recall at the meeting. If you are responsible for leading an upcoming meeting, you can

store agenda ideas in this field as well. There are numerous other examples for which you can use this text box.

- Use of Colors—Most calendar software provides the opportunity to color code your appointments. This feature allows a quick glance of your day or week and notifies you of certain appointments that are work or personal. Consider the following options:

  - Blue – All work-related items and no doubt the most frequent color;
  - Green – Personal appointments ranging from weekend activities to doctor's appointments;
  - Purple – Teaching a graduate class at a local college;
  - Yellow – "No appointment" appointments;
  - Orange – Birthdays that are recorded as daylong events; and
  - Pink – Tentative appointments that can be quickly located with a bright color.

Consider colors that make sense to you. Scan your calendar weeks in advance to schedule time for yourself and your family and color-code accordingly.

APPOINTMENT TYPES

All-Day Appointments as Reminders

Calendar software programs commonly include a feature that provides for all-day appointments. These often appear at the top of the calendar. Use this area to record any number of reminders that work in your office. Consider the following:

- Holidays—Some programs allow you to enable standard holidays in your calendar and you can add additional holidays you celebrate.
- Meetings you may or may not attend—There might be an activity planned that does not require your presence, but you want to be reminded that it will occur in case you wish to stop by if time allows.
- Vacation—Use this space to record your vacation days. It is also beneficial to record the vacation days of other team members. Your assistant can enter this information.
- Birthdays—List members of your team, your family, board member birthdays, and others that you want to remember.

Recurring Appointments

Do you hold regular meetings on the same day of the week or month? Recurring appointments are easy to enter and repeat as needed throughout your calendar. If your team meets on a monthly basis on the third Thursday of the month, it is important to record the time going forward. You can either do so manually or use the repeat feature on your software.

Another suggestion is to block the first thirty minutes of each day when possible. This commitment to the Daily Setup and a follow-up with your assistant is vital to the success of your day. If you are a leader of a team, what does this dedication of time say to others? How might you influence their daily routines? Imagine an office and team that takes the first minutes of the day to complete a Daily Setup. What might a team meeting look like if everyone had a detailed list of prioritized tasks and command of their schedules?

Tentative Appointments

The need to schedule a meeting sometimes requires you to provide several available calendar options. Create an appointment for each and do any one of the following:

- Start the title of the appointment with a question mark to indicate this time slot as a possibility;
- Use the color feature in your calendar software to shade it a color for easy identification; or
- Select from a pull-down menu of options that this appointment is "tentative."

There may be other creative ways to list tentative appointments that work for you. Sometimes, you will need to schedule another appointment on top of a tentative appointment. This technique will help to honor times that you offer to others, while also honoring the unique scheduling needs you find at any given moment. You can quickly communicate to those involved in the tentative appointment that a certain time no longer works.

No Appointment Blocking

How often do you create an appointment in your week titled "No Appointments?" Consider the fact that you need some quality work time in your office. A goal might be to schedule three "no appointment" blocks each week that each span at least two hours. Again, the time of the day depends on your schedule and preferred time of day when you are most focused. Do not leave these opportunities to chance. Each day that you find a "no appointment" in your schedule, consider tackling important tasks from your Daily Setup during that time. Treat this appointment like all others—be there on time and honor the commitment to you and your work.

Drag-and-Drop Appointments

Many software programs provide users with the ability to "drag-and-drop" an item from e-mail to create a task or calendar event. Simply drag the e-mail to the appropriate time in your calendar and an appointment will be created with a title that mirrors the e-mail's subject line. At this point, edit all fields as mentioned above to finalize. The text of the e-mail is automatically inserted in the appointment note field for retrieval later. Investigate your program to determine if this time-saving feature is possible.

DAILY PRINTOUT

After you have completed your Daily Setup, print a one-page, daily version of your calendar and task list. Many programs provide a variety of options to print daily, weekly, and monthly calendars. Why do this when you have laptop, tablet, and phone access to a calendar? There are simply times when it is not appropriate to take a device to a meeting. For example, if a client or customer is across the table and you type your notes, it can distract from the conversation. There are times when a simple portfolio and pad of paper are more appropriate for the situation.

Often, you may only need to take along your daily calendar folded in half. It gives you an overview of your day, a list of your tasks, and space to take notes if necessary. It is also a place to record future tasks and notes for use after the appointment. This list is reviewed each day during the Daily Setup and is one way to catch all the ideas and tasks you must consider throughout a day. Keep this daily printout handy and fold tomorrow's daily sheet on top of today's. At the end of the week, staple each day together and file them for future reference.

A final piece of advice: maintain only one calendar. Having to open and close this software and open another app is time-consuming and not productive. One calendar acknowledges that you have many responsibilities beyond work. Pull out your paper plate from the preface and determine if all that is on your plate is located in one calendar. The same holds true for your tasks, but we'll save that for another chapter.

While there are only twenty-four hours in a day, how you use them matters. Topics not addressed here that are equally important for your schedule are sleep, exercise, and time for nutrition. Where are family and friends in your schedule? Where are the hobbies that matter most in your schedule? A schedule can tell you a lot about a person. What does yours say?

LET'S GET STARTED!

- Conduct a time audit of your last few weeks.
- Consolidate all calendars, Post-it notes, and paper lists into one system.
- Review the appointments in your schedule over the next week and enter additional information suggested in this chapter.
- Determine frequency and enter "no appointments" appointments in your schedule.
- Conduct a conversation with those you deem appropriate regarding the changes in your schedule.

Chapter Five

Tasks

There appears to be no shortage of things to do, and the world is not slowing down. Many professionals long for the day their "to-do lists" are complete and they can, proudly, turn to a colleague and say: "Done!" Can you remember the last time you did not have multiple things to complete at once? Maybe in the third grade?

Can you list, right now, the three most important tasks you should address today? Do you have a prioritized list handy and a system in place to manage what is on your plate? Recording, tracking, and managing all that is required of you is important and leads to one recommendation: have one list. While you are a multifaceted person with many hobbies, interests, family members, and yes, a job, you should only have one list on which to record, manage, and complete *all* of your tasks. Need milk? Put it on your list. Have to write a check to the parent-teacher organization? Put it on your *one* list.

The exact type and style of your task list is your decision, but you should ask yourself these guiding questions when creating it:

- Can you access it right now?
- Is it easy to record new items or edit existing ones while on the move?
- Can you access it from multiple devices?

GETTING STARTED

A task is a single action event. When you complete the task, it is over. There are not multiple steps, phone calls, and meetings to attend to complete it. Projects and goals are made up of many tasks. Let's start with a task.

Think of all the possible times throughout your day when something comes across your desk, e-mail, or mind that needs to be completed. Look around your desk and tabletops right now. Are there papers that need to be filed or that require follow-up action from you? Review your e-mail in-box and see if there are items that need your attention or action. Tasks can arrive in many ways and from many activities. Here are some examples:

- Incoming mail—What do you do with each piece? If you subscribe to the OHIO rule (Only Handle It Once), you need to touch it once and either complete the tasks or file the item for future reference and completion.
- E-mail—How many e-mails currently reside in your in-box? Do you use your in-box as a filing system? Your goal is to find a routine that quickly changes the e-mail into a task and records it in your system for future completion.
- Phone call or Conversation—How do you record a task while engaged in a phone call or following a conversation in the office or hallway? If you agreed to do something, it must be recorded as soon as possible.
- Personal items—Where do you record family birthday reminders? What about items that need to be attended to at home? These are just as important, and should be recorded in the one master task list.

ENTERING TASKS

Throughout this book, the advice assumes you are using an electronic software program such as Microsoft Outlook or a reminder or task app. It is possible to use a paper-based platform and follow the advice presented here. However, the assumption moving forward is that you are using some sort of technology. Pick one task from any of the examples listed above and consider the following attributes when creating a task:

- Title—Limit the title of the task to as few words as possible. What is the minimum number of words needed to remind you of the task? Also, consider abbreviations that make sense to you. This is your list and it must remind you, most importantly, of what needs to be done.
- Due date or start date—Use the start date. When a task is pushed to a certain date in the future, you want to be reminded of when you should start the task. If the reminder comes on the due date, there may not be enough time for completion. Another idea is to list the due date of a project in parentheses in the title. During your Daily Setup, you will be reminded of the task on the start date you selected and the due date will be noted in the parentheses.
- Status or priority—Many software programs offer users the option to assign a status to, or prioritize a task. This is an effective tool and will be explained in more detail below.

- Reminder—This feature activates a message or alarm to remind you of the task on a certain date and time.
- Status or completion—Some programs allow you to track your progress toward completion of a task, or simply allow you to check a box when the task has been completed, removing it from your list.
- Note field (similar to the calendar note field)—This is the most underused field in the task window. If you record information in the field, place an asterisk "*" at the end of the task title. This little indication reminds you that information to help with the completion of the task is located within the note field. You may want to keep a running record of events and actions while completing the task in this area.
- Use of colors—Most calendar software programs offer a feature through which you can color-code your tasks, as described in chapter 4.

TASK PRIORITY

There are many uses for determining the priority of a task, and it needs to be a part of your Daily Setup. Pick one task from your list and ask yourself:

- How important is it?
- When is it due?
- Will I have time to complete it today?

There are numerous methods to determine a task's priority. Examples include assigning each task a letter such as A, B, or C. "A" items need to be completed today. "B" and "C" items are not urgent but may be recorded as such in a rationale that makes sense to you. Some use a simple numbering system such as 1, 2, 3, and so on. The Daily Setup described in chapter 1 suggests beginning your day with ten tasks. Of these ten, which are the most important? Simply record each with the proper label. Some programs enable you to rank order tasks from high to medium to low. If yours does not, you can simply write the proper prioritization next to each item. Consider the two suggestions above, or create a system that works for you. The goal is to start the day with a prioritized plan of action that makes it easy to determine what needs to be completed today and what to work on next.

Another tip for easy recognition is to color-code certain tasks. Again, some software allows you to assign color categories and you can determine which colors are important to you. If your system does not provide this functionality, consider printing your daily schedule and task list and simply using a highlighter. One example is to highlight all "Today" or high priority items in yellow and list a completion order for each (1, 2, 3). Next, highlight all phone calls red. This is important for recognition in both electronic and printed versions of your daily task list.

Consider how you might use the task priority option that makes sense to you. Colors also help to identify tasks and their importance. Take a few minutes now to review your list and replicate the suggestions here.

TYPES OF TASKS

Many of the tasks you complete each day are one-time, single activities. However, in every profession, there are recurring tasks that must be completed on a weekly, monthly, or yearly basis. There are also projects and goals that contain numerous tasks for completion.

Single Tasks

The simple definition of a task is that the action required for completion includes one step. Think about what you need to complete today as you are reading this book. How many tasks are single action steps? Here are several examples and suggestions:

Phone Messages

Phone calls are a part of doing business and the handling of the process is important to your credibility and your "brand." If you have a rule to return all calls within twenty-four hours, create a system that will always let you know, whether in the office or on the road. Treating phone calls and phone call messages as tasks is one way to ensure that they are handled promptly.

There is a basic set of information needed to create a task from a phone call, including the following: caller's name, phone number, and best time to return the call. You will also need any pertinent information regarding the nature of the call, in case you must prepare for the conversation or research an answer before returning the call. A good assistant will do his or her best to extrapolate as much of this information from the caller when taking the message.

When you create a task from a phone message, record the caller's phone number in the subject line. It will appear on printouts and can often be dialed from your phone by touching the number in most software programs. You can record the information related to the call in the note field mentioned above, and also color-code the phone calls within your task list, so that you can distinguish between phone calls to return and other tasks.

E-mail

One only needs to look at his or her e-mail inbox to see that e-mail has taken over as a major means of communication. Once you determine there is some action required, there are several options:

- Quick response—If you have all the information and can provide a quick response, do so. Consider the three-sentence rule—if your response is more than three sentences, pick up the phone. Imagine a world where most people adopted such a rule and stated the purpose, need, or action required in three sentences and your response was limited to three sentences as well.
- File—After reading the e-mail, you may file it away for future reference in a system of files, or you may delete the e-mail. Similar to the OHIO rule with paper, consider the benefit of handling an e-mail once and then entering it into a system that provides for later recall and action.
- Delegate—Does the e-mail need someone else's attention or action? If so, forward and provide a brief explanation (three sentences).
- Create a task—Many software programs offer a drag-and-drop feature with tasks similar to the method explained in the previous chapter with appointments. The subject of the e-mail defaults to the title of the task, and the message now appears in the note field. Determine the start date of the task and push it into the future for necessary action.

Recurring Tasks

Review your last month and identify tasks that are routine. By creating a recurring task, you create a routine that will remind you of the task—whether every Thursday or the fifteenth day of each month. Consider the following examples:

- Send board update—If you send a weekly report to your board of directors, this is a recurring task you can set as such in your software. The preparation for this task occurs throughout each week; but you can set up the task with a weekly reminder on Fridays that the report must be sent to the board that day.
- Review goals and projects—Each Wednesday, enter a reminder to review your goals and pick another day to review projects. This routine will make sure that you are reviewing your goals and projects on a weekly basis. This routine is explained in detail in chapter 10.
- Clean "Alpha Files"—As mentioned in chapter 3, Alpha Files are a great way to reduce clutter on the top of tables and in your in-basket. Create a task on the fifteenth of each month to review the files. While all actionable items in this file should be noted in your task list, there are other papers

and items that end up here. You will create a system that reminds you to review these files at least once a month; it only takes fifteen minutes!

• Positive notes—Create a recurring task to write a positive note once a week. For example, pick Wednesday and stop for a few minutes and think of someone this past week that could benefit from some words of appreciation. This task will take less than five minutes and will serve you well.

PROJECTS AND GOALS

While this may appear to be an unusual recommendation, record your goals and projects in your task list. While the explanation above clearly delineates the difference between a single action task and multiple-step projects and goals, you need one place to locate everything. While a separate list somewhere else may work for you, try the suggestion to place both your goals and projects in your task list. The description on how to enter goals and projects is listed below. A routine to review your goals and projects on a weekly basis, as part of your Daily Setup, is explained in chapter 10.

GOALS

Goals are an important part of your career and life aspirations. You probably have goals that are required at work, form the basis of your annual evaluation, and impact your compensation. There are also other professional goals relating to where you want to be in five or ten years. You should have personal goals that focus on topics such as family, health, spirituality, or gratitude. What are your goals? Can you list them? Do you have a system in place that allows you to review them on a routine basis?

Goals must be recorded as a task and the first step is creating the title, which can be as simple as a word or two to remind you of the goal. For example: Compensation Study, Communications, Program Evaluation Tool, and Capital Project Plan. At this point, all you need is a title for your goal.

Next, record the goal as a task in your software. The only difference is the prefix used to offset this as a goal instead of a single task. Begin the title with the word "GOAL" in all capital letters and then list the title of the goal. Here are several examples:

• GOAL: Compensation Study
• GOAL: Program Evaluation Tool
• GOAL: Communications

The capital letters help to recognize this is a goal and not a single task. Some software will also allow a color-coding of certain tasks to allow for visual recognition of the goal.

Next, begin to brainstorm all the various steps, deadlines, and assistance of others required to achieve the goal. Don't worry at this point about what comes first or second, just list all the things currently on your mind that you will need to complete. Consider the steps you personally need to complete, steps that others need to complete and that should be delegated, and other research and people to contact. Remember, all goals move forward one task at a time. As you revisit your goal each week, you will update your progress and edit the list of tasks moving forward.

The final step in creating the task is to select a start date to begin. You have successfully taken one goal and entered it into your system. Here is an example from one goal (above) that includes a title, various action steps, and two deadlines:

- GOAL: Compensation Study

  - Complete a thorough review of compensation for personnel and pro-vide recommendations by March 15, 2016.

    - Gather current salary matrix
    - Review last five years of salary matrices
    - Investigate companies to conduct salary study
    - Review comparable salaries in our field regionally
    - Review comparative salaries outside of our field regionally
    - Prepare final recommendations by February 1

As you make progress and review your goal, you will certainly think of other tasks to list and maybe a couple of tasks that are no longer relevant.

Please take a few minutes right now to list your goals in a similar fashion and enter them in your system. Start listing your work goals for the year and finish with personal goals. It is equally important for you as a human to think holistically about your place in the world. Is there a desire to advance your education? Create the goal and brainstorm the list of action steps in the note field. Would you like to write a book or learn how to play the piano? List the goals and action steps right now. Completing this simple step will put you on a better track to make progress as opposed to just dreaming about a possibility.

PROJECTS

A project involves more than one single-action task. Take a look at your task list. Can you determine which items are single tasks and which are projects? Making a phone call to schedule car maintenance is a single task that may be checked off when completed. Completing a state report might not be so simple. For example, you might need to gather historical data from previous years, call the state to clarify items, and consult with team members on various project components.

The first step toward recording your project in your task list is to create a title for the project. For the example provided above, it would look like this:

• PROJECT: State Report (3/15)

The capital letters stand out and easily indicate the item is a multiple-step project. The parenthetical notation of March 15 indicates the due date.

Your next step is to immediately brainstorm all that is needed to complete the project. Write each step in the note field. Don't worry that you might not have all the steps at this moment; as you complete steps, other steps may be apparent and need to be added in the note field. As you review this project on a weekly basis, you will edit as you see necessary. The completion of the example project might look like this:

• PROJECT: State Report (3/15)

  • Gather last three years of reports
  • Review prior reports
  • Call state for clarification on deadline
  • Gather data from team (Jill, Michael, Sally)
  • Complete report online by March 1

Take a few minutes to review your tasks and begin to set up projects. Remember that tasks are single-action items and should be listed as such. Projects contain multiple steps and need to be recorded and reviewed differently from tasks.

Task completion is important to all leaders and demonstrates your ability to manage and deliver on promises and expectations. This chapter recommends a routine manner to look at tasks, recurring tasks, goals, and projects. What insight can you take away right now to create an approach to completing tasks that works for you?

LET'S GET STARTED!

- Review and reflect on your current method for recording and completing tasks.
- Research a system that enables you to record tasks along with start dates, priorities, and a note field.
- Take one task at a time and record it in your system.
- Take one goal or project and record it in your system.
- Review your responsibilities for recurring tasks and enter them as such.
- Conduct a conversation with your assistant regarding the changes in your management of tasks.

Chapter Six

Note Taking

Meetings are a routine part of our lives. There is much written about the productivity, cost, or frustration of meetings in books and journals. Let's face it, they are a necessary component of any business, organization, or group—even a family. There are days and weeks when we seem to travel from one meeting to another or meet with direct reports one after the other. Unless you have superhuman memory skills, information and details seem to run together after a while. The ability to capture notes and details is important. What is your note-taking system? Where do you write the necessary items for recall and for follow-up action? Where do you file the notes when meetings end? Why? Because there is another meeting in ten minutes!

Take a look at others sitting in your next meeting. How are they taking notes? Chances are, some will be writing notes on paper, some will be using technology, and some will be staring "out there" instead of taking notes. The two options for note taking discussed here will include using paper and technology. Both forms are effective and the choice is yours to make prior to each meeting. Before exploring each, consider the following section on technology use during meetings.

At your next meeting, you will likely see someone typing away on a laptop or tablet. Have you ever wondered what they were really doing? Taking notes? Responding to e-mail? The truth is, no one really knows! There are times when using technology to take notes during a meeting is not appropriate. Here are some examples of why technology use in a meeting is a bad idea:

- Engagement—Using technology to take notes makes others question what you are really doing on the device in front of you. Determine whether the need to save notes in a digital form is necessary. If so, and it is the culture of your office or team, continue. If not, ask yourself if it is worth the risk of appearing distracted or disengaged throughout a team meeting.

- Keyboard flak—Listen to your typing in the privacy and quiet of your office. Can you hear the keyboard flak? There is always a little noise and some keyboards and keyboard strokes are downright loud. Decide if this is appropriate in a meeting.
- Meeting climate—Sitting across from an angry parent or team member is difficult. Ask yourself if you really need a device between you and them. Do you need to peck away at notes while they share their experience? Are you proficient enough that you can maintain eye contact and continue to type notes? What if you were the one expressing concern and the other person was typing away? Try to imagine what that looks like from the other side of the table. At moments like these, it is best to bring your portfolio with a paper tablet and take notes.

PAPER

Paper-based note taking can appear in a variety of styles and sizes to fit most any need. There are planners on the market that fit any number of paper sizes, from legal- to coat pocket-size. Determine what your needs are beyond the typical meeting and the need for portability.

- Planners—If you use a Day Timer or Franklin Covey planner system, there is paper within your tool to use in a meeting. In a daily view planner, there often is an opposite page specifically for taking notes from your day. There is also a space in the back of such planners that contains additional blank pages.
- Portfolios—All executives need to have several portfolios at their disposal. When it is time for the next meeting, it is a simple grab-and-go. Place extra portfolios in your car and home office when you attend a meeting first thing in the morning.
- Note-Taking Forms—There are single sheets of paper that are formatted for taking meeting notes. They can be found in the planners mentioned above. Conduct research and find one that works for you. The other option is to create one from a number of styles available. There is an example of a note form in appendix A that incorporates the following features:

  - Meeting Title—This is simply the title that corresponds to the meeting and also the file in which this form will eventually be placed.
  - Date—Simply enter the date of the meeting.
  - Start Time and End Time—Again, for documentation purposes, simply list the start and end time of the meeting.

- Present and Absent—Record who attended the meeting and who was absent.
- Action Items—As you move through the meeting, record two items here: (1) Your tasks—If you committed to a task, immediately list it, add your name and the due date. (2) Others' tasks—If someone in the meeting committed to a task, record it and his or her name. If you are the CEO, recording team members' task due dates is an effective way to manage the team.
- Communication Task—Similar to an action item, this section asks the following question: As a result of this meeting, what do we need to communicate? Decisions, next actions, or future meeting dates are all important. This section clarifies communication tasks, assigns responsibility and provides due dates. This question can be asked in real time during the meeting or as a summary at the end.
- Meeting Notes—The form provides roughly a page and a half to record any notes from the meeting.

- Inside Sheets—The following two forms are used as part of the daily calendar printout each day. The two pages have different uses but are always folded inside the daily calendar that you should carry with you each day. Full-page examples of each are located in appendix A.

  - Cabinet, Board, or Meeting Management Inside Sheet—This page is broken into three parts: (1) Cabinet—As superintendent, you often have a cabinet made up of your direct reports. The top section of the form is space to list topics of discussion for those on your team. You might be in the middle of another meeting when an idea pops into your head. Record it here, on your inside sheet, for later discussion with the appropriate team member. Adapt this section to meet your needs and the number of team members you want to list, and change the title to the person's name. Another use is to take the last two lines under each person and briefly list yearly goals. This section will be extremely beneficial when we discuss weekly meetings in chapter 9. (2) Board— Use this space to record topics to include in your weekly update. Again, you might be in the middle of a meeting and a discussion topic is one that you should share with the board. Immediately record the topic in this section and you will be reminded of it when creating your weekly update. There are also sections for topics relating to your solicitor, board president, and agenda items for future board leadership meetings and board workshops. (3) Meeting Management—The bottom half of the sheet is used to help manage the meetings for which you are responsible and to record meeting agenda items. Again, you may be in a meeting regarding a new federal mandate and want to review it with

your team. Enter a brief description of the topic; when it is time to build
the upcoming meeting agenda, simply refer to your inside sheet, where
you've recorded suggestions for agenda topics.

- Rolling Three-Month Board Meeting Sheet—If you are responsible for
  monthly meetings, this form will provide a three-month rolling overview of the various parts of the meetings. The sheet provides spaces to
  record any workshop topics, your administrative report ideas, discussion items, action items, or executive sessions for each of the three
  months into the future.

Paper is still relevant in this digital era and will always play a part in an
overall system of organization. Inside sheets are excellent ways to capture all
the thoughts, ideas, agenda items, or discussion topics that you are responsible for and are part of managing your merry-go-round. It provides a place
to record and access details to create the agenda for a meeting with your
leadership team, topics for a meeting with a direct report, or a list of board
meeting discussion items. Imagine what your next meeting will look like
with a meeting note form and inside sheets ready to record important information and deadlines.

DIGITAL

The world is making use of the digital revolution and innovations roll out
weekly to improve productivity. Trying to implement each new product or
application is a full-time job. There are certainly benefits to using technology
to record meetings, goals, or ideas in general. Applications like Evernote and
Notability are widely used and well known for these purposes; regardless of
the application used, there are distinct advantages to such software.

- Access—Once you create an account, you are able to access your notes
  from a desktop or laptop, tablet, or smartphone. Regardless of where you
  find yourself, if you think of an idea or a need to talk with someone about
  a certain topic, you can access your notes.
- One-Stop Shop—Consider this your one-stop shop for everything on your
  plate. You can list your professional work goals, books to read, groceries
  to purchase for the week, and many other possibilities that help you keep it
  all together and in one place.
- Availability—As you read a book, listen to an audio podcast in the car, or
  watch a late night movie, you may have an idea for a future meeting or
  presentation. If your smartphone is nearby, you can simply record the idea
  and return to the movie. These applications provide 24/7 access to your
  lists.

- Collaboration—Technology provides access to shared notes. If your team is working on a project, create a shared note for others to reference and contribute to going forward. Also, consider your assistant and the access it provides him or her to certain notes.
- Visual Record—If you are in a meeting typing notes on your laptop, and want to take a picture of the brainstorm diagram on the whiteboard, simply open the note on your phone and snap a picture. You now have an image to refer to after the meeting.
- Search Capabilities—You are able to conduct a keyword search of your notes from meetings, conferences, or goals and quickly locate information.
- Audio Record—Some programs allow you to record a meeting or add a voice memo as you debrief. If it is a shared note, others can provide status updates via an audio recording.
- E-mail—Certain programs create a unique e-mail address to mail blog posts, Web site links, and other content to your account. There may be an article that you want to share with your team at the next meeting. E-mail the article to your account and access it later, from any device, as you build your agenda.
- Goals and Projects—Digital note taking allows you to track updates and progress on your goals in one place. Simply create a note, and track your activity related to goals and projects. If it is a shared note, others can contribute to the overall progress of the goal or project.

There are other programs available that provide for sketching and note taking on a tablet. This allows for a creative form of note taking and blends both a keyboard and a stylus. For the more artistic, this includes color choices and a visual way to depict notes and communicate. Consider asking your team to read an article and prepare a visual representation to share with others at a team meeting. There is no one way to take notes, and using any number of apps on the market will provide a fresh approach.

One final recommendation is to use the note field in a task or scheduled appointment. It is a text box that allows you to keep track of activity regarding a task or details of a meeting. It is also accessible after the meeting and can be printed for filing. As mentioned before, the note field for both tasks and appointments is underused. Open one today and consider how you might record information in this space.

When you are superintendent, meetings are critical to the information flow to you and from others on your team. How you take notes during a meeting—and how your team members take notes—will determine the effectiveness of the meeting and, often, the success of post-meeting actions. There is much coming at you each day, too much in fact to remember it all. A routine system for taking, storing, and recalling notes will assist you and your effectiveness.

LET'S GET STARTED!

- Decide when it is appropriate to use technology in a meeting and when it is not.
- Gather a few portfolios for the office, car, and home.
- Create or purchase note-taking forms.
- Review and test various note-taking apps and find the one that fits your style.

Chapter Seven

Delegation

What is your job? Really—what exactly is a superintendent supposed to do? Think about what you did yesterday. Last week. Were you doing your job? Did you look busy and have little time for others? Is busy your job? Certainly you have witnessed superintendents or bosses throughout your career. Are you doing what they did and behaving as they modeled for you? Most importantly, what do you say during your visit to the second-grade classroom when, after being introduced, a child in the front row asks, "What is a superintendent?"

Take a few minutes now and find a piece of scratch paper. List the three to five "big rocks" or responsibilities of the superintendent. Now, go find a copy of your job description. Certainly you saw it when they offered you the job . . . right? Compare your three to five items with those listed on your job description.

- Are there similarities?
- Are there differences?
- Are you doing the work as designed by the job description? Or
- Are you doing the job as modeled for you over the years and what you think you should be doing each day?

What have you learned as a result of this exercise? If you are comfortable enough, go ahead and share this with a trusted colleague. Consider conducting this same exercise with your board. Ask them to list three to five responsibilities that they believe should be your priorities. Then pass out your job description and see what happens. Maybe there is congruence with the findings. Maybe, just maybe, this could lead to a conversation that provides clarity for leaders of the district. What do you think the community's perception of what the superintendent's job is? Teachers, faculty, and staff? And don't forget the second-grade students!

Once you have some direction on what your job is and what you must do, consider conducting a similar activity with your cabinet. Ask them during a cabinet meeting to list the three to five biggest responsibilities that define their positions and provide a few minutes for think time. When ready, pass out each person's job description, have him or her compare, and ask them similar questions to the ones listed above for you.

Ask them to reflect on the activity and come prepared to your next weekly meeting (with just the two of you) with some feedback on the exercise. Be prepared to calibrate their perceived "big rocks" with what the district expects and needs, the job description and your expectations. Perhaps this activity will reveal the need to alter job descriptions. It might also result in scrapping existing descriptions and starting fresh. Times have changed yet in many cases job descriptions, if you can find them, have not.

Knowing what your job consists of is important. What is it that you, and only you, can do? This simple question starts the foundation of what *you must do* versus what *you can delegate to others*. This is a critical step in your organization. It starts with you but leads to conversations with your team members and discussions about their essential functions. These conversations create a clearer picture of who does what and where you can turn for assistance in completing all that is required of you.

DELEGATION

A common struggle for superintendents is moving from doing the day-to-day responsibilities of a previous job to that of being the superintendent, or the person responsible for everything in the district. If you are making the transition successfully, there will be days where it seems that all you do is assign tasks and check on tasks that need to be completed. This might be relative to the size of your district and those who report directly to you. Regardless, it is a skill that you need to master.

Delegation is important for several reasons:

- Your job is to do the types of tasks required of a superintendent or the CEO. If you are doing the work of others or work that is familiar from your last position, chances are there is not enough time to do *your* work and you likely spend evenings and weekends working. This is not healthy, nor is it a productive long-term strategy.
- It provides for the growth of those who report to you. Your job is to help your team members grow, and prepare them for the next steps in their

careers. You should assign tasks that foster growth and provide the opportunity to experience both success and failure that results in the process.

- It provides for your sanity and ability to manage the district. If you desire to be a leader, you must manage the day-to-day routine items of a district. Your success in the role of the superintendency is important to the employees who count on you to be their leader, count on you to provide a stable workplace, and count on their job for the financial means to support their family. Your family is also counting on you as well.

What to Delegate?

Think of all the routine items that you complete each day as a start for possible tasks to delegate. Are there routine forms that are usually signed by you that others could sign? Consider such items as requests for time off, leaves of absence, graduate course forms, educational field trip forms, and budget expenditures. If you calculated your hourly rate, as suggested in chapter 2, is this the best use of your time? How can you delegate such items to your assistant and others on your team? Just because the previous superintendent signed each educational trip form does not mean it must continue. While it is important to manage the overall district budget, is it necessary to approve purchases that were budgeted for and approved by a principal and the business manager?

Other areas to consider delegating are tasks that are not your strong suit or that you don't want to complete. These decisions are made following the activities mentioned above and a clear understanding of job responsibilities on your team.

HOW TO DELEGATE

There are several steps to delegating a task to another person on your team or your assistant that work well with the system of creating and entering tasks outlined in this book. First and foremost, a task that is delegated to a colleague needs to be entered into your task list for future recall. You are ultimately responsible for everything, including the task you just asked someone else to complete. Therefore, it needs to be recorded in your system. If you are the type of manager that assigns work and never follows up, it is probable that members of your team know this and respond accordingly.

Steps to delegate

1. Determine the task. You must be clear about exactly what it is that needs to be completed. Is it a task or a project? This distinction, as

mentioned in chapter 5, is important for you to know so you can determine whether it is a single action item or a multistep project.

2. Determine time needed for completion. You need to manage the task from your perspective. When is the task or project due from you? Begin planning backward from this date and communicate the time frame with plenty of lead-time. There may be additional work on your end once the task is completed and returned to you. Also, consider building in time to review and redirect efforts, if necessary. Provide yourself with the necessary time to review, redirect, and then complete the task that is on your plate.

3. Determine which team member is best suited to complete the task. There are several variables.

   - Job description: Who has the responsibility to complete such a request as per their job description? This is usually the go-to person.
   - Experience: Does someone on your team have experience with the type of request?
   - Growth opportunity: Might this delegation be an opportunity to stretch and grow a member of your team?
   - Their plate: Before delegating an item to a team member, consider what else is currently on that member's plate. Is this a busy time of the year or are they stretched a little thin at the moment? Do they have a vacation scheduled in the next couple of weeks?
   - More than one person: Consider assigning a task or a project to more than one person. If collaboration is part of your culture, how can you engage two or three team members in the completion of a task or project? It eliminates a single point of failure and creates a culture of working together and supporting each other on deadlines and requests.

4. Communicate the task, with two considerations in mind: how and when.

   - How to communicate about the task: As simple as this sounds, what is the best way to ask, suggest, or direct a member on your team to do something? Do you march into the office and direct them to do such-and-such by the end of the week? Or might you state that you need their help on a project and request them to complete a few items for you? There will be times when you do this a lot, and your approach as the boss means more than you probably know. Think back to your journey and how your boss once delegated to you.

There is no "right" way to delegate a task and no "one" way to treat all employees.

- When to communicate about the task: If you follow the advice and routines in this book, there will be numerous times to delegate a task. There are weekly private meetings with cabinet members, weekly cabinet meetings with the entire team, and other such opportunities throughout the week. Determine what might be the best time—alone or in front of the team. Again, there is no "one" way to have a delegation conversation.

5. Seek clarity after communicating with your colleague.

- After the task is communicated, it is important to make sure your colleague is clear about what is expected and by when. There is no doubt you understand the request, but are you sure the other person does?
- It is also good to discuss if there is anything that will prevent completion of the task at the agreed upon time. Do they have too much on their plate and would they even tell you? Are they scheduled to attend a conference or take a vacation in the coming week?

6. Ask if any assistance is needed.

- An excellent question to ask is if the receiver of the delegated task needs some help to complete the task. This conversation might lead to assigning the task to another colleague or providing some assistance. Also ask if there is there anything you can do to clear a path to assist with completion.

7. Record the delegated task in your task list. This is the critical part and a game-changer for most. Where do you record, right now, all the things you ask of others? Is there a separate list, or perhaps you rely on your good old faithful memory? The following steps should look similar to recording a task as reviewed in chapter 5:

- Name the task—Using as few words as possible, list the task that you just handed off to a colleague.
- Indicate it is a delegated task—Use a capital "W" following the task title. This will clearly indicate that you are waiting for the task.
- List the name—Following the "W," list the team member's name who is responsible for the task.
- Due date—List the date when the task is due back to you in parentheses at the end of the title.

- Push—Push the task into the future to be reminded of the assignment during your Daily Setup with the following two considerations:
- Due date—If you have time and believe the team member will complete the project with little to no oversight, you can push to the date agreed upon for completion.
- Calibration date—If you want to check in with the team member prior to the due date, push the task as far out as you feel comfortable. You may want to check on the project in as little as a couple of days to a week into the project to assure clarity and progress on completion. You will learn from experience about who on your team needs a little more oversight than others.

8. Check in—There are times in your routine meetings each week, weeklies, and cabinet meetings to check on the status of various delegated tasks. It might be appropriate to ask about an item during cabinet, if there are others assigned to the task, or you might do so privately during a weekly one-on-one meeting.
9. Rewarding success—Consider how you thank members of your team and express your appreciation for a job well done. While they do any number of tasks and projects for the district, you should take time to say thank you publicly and privately.

Delegation is critical to your success and the success of those on your team. Try as you might, you can't do it all. The members of your team are there to assist and perform their critical job functions and they are counting on you to do yours.

LET'S GET STARTED

- Conduct the activity regarding your perceived responsibilities and those on your job description.
- Conduct a similar activity with your cabinet.
- Review your task list daily for items that might be delegated.
- Delegate a task and use the guidance above to record it in your system for follow-up.

Part Two

Weekly Routines

In part 2, we will turn our attention toward weekly routines. One example is weekly meetings with your team members. These sessions enable you to better understand the pulse of the organization and identify which tasks need to be completed on a weekly basis. How can you maximize these routines to become a better leader? The first chapter in part 2 presents the "weekly review," a routine that provides for a review of the current week, a look ahead three weeks into your schedule, and a preview of the next three months' worth of tasks. These weekly routines provide a cadence that you and members of your team will come to rely on as a normal part of the week.

Chapter Eight

The Weekly Review

Dealing with your various day-to-day meetings and priorities can make each day feel like it runs right into the next. Leaders need to stop at least once a week and take stock of where they are and where they need to go in order to accomplish their goals. If you don't schedule this weekly review with yourself, you will wake up and wonder where the days, weeks, or even months have gone.

The weekly review is the time to examine your schedule and task list, either by yourself or with others. Scheduling this time will help you manage and lead more effectively, particularly because the weekly review:

- Creates a routine appointment each week;
- Encourages weekly reflection; and
- Slows the merry-go-round and provides greater control of your schedule and your life.

Start by setting aside an hour for the weekly review. Close your door, announce to others what you are doing, and why. The rest of this chapter provides you with guidance on how to set up your weekly review. After a few weeks of implementation, you will look forward to this time to review, recharge, and recommit.

PICK THE DAY

The day of the week to schedule your weekly review is up to you. There are five days each week and the exact day is your choice, but the important thing is that you stick with the routine you establish. Here is the case for three of the days:

- Monday—The beginning of the week is a great time to conduct a weekly review because it enables you to stand in front of your workweek. As you review your calendar and tasks, you can preview your week and make commitments for the coming week. For some, this provides a focus and kick-start to the week. It also provides an opportunity to review the previous week and note any outstanding items or tasks that need to be added to this week's schedule.
- Wednesday—Scheduling a review in the middle of the week gives you the opportunity to look backward and forward at the same time. In the middle of the week, ask yourself what have you accomplished since last Wednesday and what you need to accomplish by the next Wednesday.
- Friday—If you plan your weekly review for the end of the week, you give yourself time to stop the whirlwind and end the week with reflection. What successes have you accomplished over the last week? What impact will this week's activities have on next week? A Friday review allows for closure for the week and a clear head entering the weekend.

Do you travel often or are there certain days that might not work for a weekly review? Try out the days suggested above and see what works for you. The goal is to pick one that does, form a routine and stick to it.

ATTENDEES

You are the main attendee at each of your weekly review meetings, but there are times when you may want to invite colleagues to join you for part of a meeting for various reasons. Consider the following suggestions when setting up your weekly review:

- You—The minimum requirement is you. The weekly review is really about you, your schedule, and all that is required of you personally and professionally. At the very least, do this with yourself once a week. Consider starting out by yourself and practice the routine for a couple of weeks. This will allow you to smooth out any kinks and develop a rhythm that can be shared with others.
- Your Assistant—A weekly review that involves your assistant is a commitment to a scheduled time to meet one-on-one with a critical member of your team. As mentioned in chapter 1, you should touch base with your assistant following your Daily Setup. The weekly review provides a scheduled time with your assistant to discuss the overall functionality of the relationship and your office.
- Others—Consider if it makes sense for others to join the review. Some possibilities might include a communications director or other key mem-

bers on your team who need to know your schedule and priorities. There may be times to invite someone to review and discuss a major project impacting his or her area of responsibility. It is also a great way to teach others the power of the weekly review.

THE PROCESS

Establishing a process for your weekly review that you can follow each meeting will help you use your time most effectively. Once you have decided on a process, each weekly review will flow the same way, allowing you to move from item to item efficiently.

The first step is to review your calendar from the previous week. This may occur with either paper copies of your week-at-a-view or an electronic version. Begin with each day and review your past appointments. Ask yourself the following questions:

- What follow-up tasks might there be to complete?
- Are there any thank-you letters I need to write?
- How many appointments were there and am I happy with the number and flow of the previous week?

There are often appointments that will recur. Use this time to review the success of each and make plans to improve. For example, a board meeting or workshop held last week should be reviewed. If there was a leadership team meeting last week, how did it go? What ways can you and your office improve before the next meeting? This is the perfect time to review these and other events with your assistant.

The next step is to review your calendar three weeks into the future. Review each appointment and discuss any preparation needed. Some examples:

- Are there agendas that need to be completed? Once completed, review with your assistant and discuss the distribution process.
- Are there food and beverage requirements? Note these and make any preparations you can or schedule for follow-up closer to the date.
- Take note of any travel in your schedule and prepare accordingly. Do you need directions to a meeting? Are there other "out of the office" travel arrangements that either need to be made or reviewed?
- Is there enough travel time between each appointment? Consider placing travel time in your calendar and treat that as part of the appointment.
- Review evening appointments and prepare for times when there is no office support in the building.

- Are you attending a conference or meeting? Review registration for meetings and conferences and any travel assistance you might need.
- Review appointments and time slots that still appear as "tentative." You may have reserved several dates for a possible meeting. The weekly review will keep a three-week watch on these and help you clean up your schedule at least once a week.
- Review and schedule time for "no appointments." This provides time to close your door to work on projects and priorities.

As you work the process week after week and develop a rhythm, you will never have an appointment sneak up on you. While there will be an overlap in the review of a few weeks, the system provides a routine review of your schedule. If you change your schedule while away from the office or in a meeting, you can review the change upon your return, or you will catch it during your weekly review. If your assistant handles the scheduling of appointments for you, the weekly review provides time to review those changes.

The next step is to review the upcoming three months of tasks on your task list. The formation of a monthly task list will be covered in chapter 12. Most jobs have cyclical items that need to be completed during certain times of the year. Take this time to review the next three months and add any items to your task list. There may be "beginning of a school year" tasks or items to close out the school year. Take each item and enter it into your task list software and schedule the start dates as far out as necessary.

Finally, review your in-basket and process any loose items that need to be removed and filed. Review your task list with your assistant. Discuss your workload and your assistant's workload and plan accordingly. This is a weekly appointment with yourself and your assistant that is critical to your success. Ask your assistant for feedback regarding the flow of work and the relationship in general. Ask him or her what you could do to improve the working relationship in the office.

After you complete the weekly review for several weeks, you will benefit from a rhythm that minimizes urgency and provides plenty of notice of your appointments and commitments. One rule on most teams and with your assistant: No surprises. A weekly review will provide the routine to minimize these occurrences.

LET'S GET STARTED!

- Select a day of the week to hold a weekly review and schedule it.
- Conduct several weekly reviews by yourself.
- Invite your assistant, and perhaps others, to your weekly review.
- Share the process with others on your team.

Chapter Nine

Weekly Meetings

Your daily schedule fills up for any number of reasons. There are pop-up meetings, emergencies, phone calls, and e-mails to answer. While you must account for these in your day, there is a better way to fill your daily schedule to help manage and prioritize your responsibilities. Reflecting on the past couple of weeks in your schedule, what do you see or notice? What patterns and trends emerge? The appointments that you see are only the ones that were scheduled, but we all know there were other interruptions to your day.

The weekly review—detailed in the previous chapter—is an opportunity for you to review your schedule and ask your assistant for input from his or her perspective. If an assistant manages your schedule, she or he will have firsthand knowledge of how easy or difficult it is to find room to create appointments in your calendar.

RHYTHM OF CONVERSATIONS

While the advent of virtual meetings is upon us, there is nothing that replaces a face-to-face, one-on-one conversation in your office with the door closed. Here, your presence sends a clear message about what is important to you. Sound bites such as phone calls, e-mails, and brief chats in the hallway are not effective communication tools when it comes to building a relationship with your team members. Expecting important organizational goals to move forward on their own without the rhythm of face-to-face conversations is leaving too much to chance. Obviously, in large global organizations this is difficult. In a local school district, personal time is both possible and essential.

Take a look at your week and the number of people who report directly to you. What meetings should you schedule weekly to stay in touch with the organization? Factors to consider are the number of direct reports, the time of the day, the duration of the meeting, and the day of the week. Let's take a look at each one:

- Number of direct reports—This number will vary according to the organization size. There may be as few as two to three or closer to ten. This will factor into the amount of time available and should be considered in your schedule. Refer to your organization chart to make sure it is accurate.
- Time of day—When is it best for you to meet with others and be truly present and focused? There are early morning people and others who hit their strides in the afternoon. Knowing yourself is critical to your leadership success and to the success of others. If you know you need a couple of hours and some coffee to truly be present, schedule them in the late morning or early afternoon. If you are at all confused as to what is your best time, ask your assistant or others on your team. If they feel comfortable enough to be honest with you, they will tell you.
- Duration—Depending on the number of people you need to see in a week, the duration might need to be altered. Start with an hour as a base and adjust accordingly. The more people you have on your list, the less time you might schedule. This will be determined by your individual circumstances.
- Day of the week—There are options here that need to be considered with what your typical weekly calendar looks like. Is there more time at the beginning, middle, or end of the week to conduct one-on-one meetings? Depending on the number, you might spread them out or pick an afternoon and conduct several back-to-back. You may want to consider scheduling them either at the beginning or end of the week.

The important point of weekly one-on-ones is the time you create to meet personally with each team member. This rhythm will become a natural part of your schedule, and that of your direct reports. They will trust this is sacred time to discuss important items. Consider the options above and begin. You can modify as you experiment with times, duration, or days of the week.

WEEKLY ONE-ON-ONES

Why Weeklies?

- Knowledge—As the superintendent, there is just too much information for one person to handle effectively. Weekly meetings provide a snapshot into your direct reports' areas of responsibility and enough information to be knowledgeable about those responsibilities. There are times when the situation or issue requires a deeper dive into the facts and history. How will you know when this is necessary? Holding weekly meetings is the best way to stay informed about potential issues that you are ultimately responsible for and you need to manage.

- Pulse—Every organization has a pulse or rhythm. How do you currently detect the pulse across the buildings, functions, and people you lead? Meeting weekly with key team members provides you with insight into these areas and more.
- Dashboard—Your command of the organization could be viewed as a dashboard with certain indicators. Where are things progressing well and what areas need more attention?
- Praise, tune, redirect—This private meeting is an excellent opportunity to say thank you or great job between just the two of you. While there are times that it is appropriate for a large group acknowledgment, sitting in your office with direct eye contact is a golden opportunity to acknowledge your team member in person. This meeting also provides moments to fine tune or redirect efforts.
- Face time—As the boss, you are busy and pulled in multiple directions and meetings. How visible are you? How hard is it for your team members to find a few minutes of time with you? When your direct reports know they have a standing opportunity to meet and speak with you weekly, they will scale back the "Hey—do you have a minute?" visits to your office. When you are the boss, never forget what it was like when you weren't. Never forget what it meant to you when the boss took time out to meet with you, praise you, direct you, or engage with just you.

Agenda for Weeklies

Whatever the length of your weeklies, there should be a rhythm to these meetings. They occur in your office with your door closed. As always, your assistant will know when to interrupt, but the focus is on the other person and their time with you. As you welcome them into your office, here is some advice:

- Begin with a question—An agenda might be useful but it is not necessary. Start off the meeting with a question—what is the first thing we should be talking about today? Sit back and let your team member start and guide the conversation. There may be an item that they have held off bothering you with, but which needs some direction or clarification from you. Allow them to review their list of items first. If you do this every time, they will come prepared to discuss a larger issue first.
- Be prepared with your list—Do you have a list of topics to discuss with your direct report right now? Take the advice you are giving your team

members and maintain a list of items you wish to discuss at the weekly meeting with them. When the appointed weekly begins, you too have a list to review. If anything is urgent, address it immediately. This becomes known as "Your List/My List" and becomes part of the meeting culture.

- Bring your inside sheet—This was explained in chapter 6, but it is important to review again. The top half of the sheet provides space to record items to discuss for each direct report, either under their name or title. This is the ideal time to pull out your inside sheet and review your items. This sheet is folded underneath your daily calendar printout and is with you all day. When an idea for discussion with a direct report pops into your head, record it immediately. When the weekly meeting arrives, you have your list of items to discuss as well. The full-page view of an inside sheet is located in appendix A.
- Review goals—Each week, you have the opportunity to check in and discuss progress on your direct reports' goals. This attention to detail is rare and is invaluable to the overall progress of the organization. An essential question to ask: What needs to occur over the next week to move their goal forward? Once you and your colleague agree upon the next step, record it, and commit to talking about it next week.
- Have a conversation—Remember, this is also an opportunity to talk about your team member's world outside of work. Do you know much about their family? Hobbies? Continuing education? Life is short. Take an interest in people beyond the job. Ask about their kids. Ask about their significant others. Ask about their hopes and dreams. Remember to share a little about you.

WEEKLY CABINET MEETINGS

As important as it is to meet one-on-one with your key team members, it is just as important to meet with the team as a whole. A weekly cabinet meeting promotes communication and collaboration and demonstrates your dedication to teamwork. The routine of a weekly cabinet meeting offers your team an opportunity to bring an idea or issue to the team. As they examine their task lists, and review their goals and projects, they know there is a standing meeting where "all hands are on deck" to listen and provide feedback.

The membership in this meeting is your decision. Consider your direct reports, and determine how many team members comprise that group. Three is a good minimum, and most districts have at least three administrators working at the district level. From there, you can build the team. There are times when team members other than direct reports should attend. For example, the director of building and grounds is a critical person on your team. However, this individual also reports to the business manager. Are you satisfied with the business manager representing and speaking on behalf of building and grounds? If so, you may decide not to include the director of building and grounds.

Make sure to clearly communicate your expectations to the group regarding attendance and participation. Do you consider their attendance essential and wish absences to be minimal? If the meeting is important enough to have, and you believe in collaboration, set the expectation that this weekly standing appointment is mandatory. Hold the meeting at the same time each week and have people place the meetings on their schedules at the beginning of the school year.

As a superintendent, one of your major responsibilities is to manage and lead public meetings. Whether you have one board meeting or several, these are public performances that require many parts of the school district to communicate and collaborate. Weekly team meetings provide an opportunity for you to review the last board meeting and to identify any follow-up actions required of you and your team.

Questions to ask at the cabinet meeting include:

- What went well last night?
- What needs to be improved?
- After a review of each agenda item, what follow-up tasks do we have?
- Who will take responsibility for each task?
- What is the deadline for completion of each task?
- What follow-up communication tasks are there?
- What implications are there for the next meeting?

A cabinet meeting is also a time to prepare for the next board meeting, whether it is next week or next month. In chapter 12, the monthly task list will demonstrate how board action items that are routine may become part of your planning routine. If there is a financial item that needs approval, review that with your business manager. If there are curriculum items for approval next month, review the status with your assistant superintendent. Will there be a public presentation about student learning that involves teachers and students? Who will handle the logistics? As you begin to embrace the routine of these meetings, you will come to rely on weekly cabinet meetings to prepare for board meetings and other events in the normal course of the year.

DISCOURSE

So what will the meeting actually look like and who will say what? How will the meeting look if it did not follow a board meeting? There are many ideas and suggestions in the research regarding effective ways to hold weekly status meetings. What is important is that the group is involved in the design, is expected to contribute, and periodically stops and discusses their effectiveness as a group. Not everyone on your team is alike. Some will talk more and some will talk less. Your job is to create a structure that will enable all to participate and feel comfortable joining in during the meeting. Here are three suggestions for facilitating discussion within your meeting:

1. Name your three items or big rocks—Begin with one person and continue around the table so that each member of your team shares three big rocks or items on their list. These can be goals, projects, or tasks on their plate at the moment. It is important to make this a routine each week so your team members can come prepared with their three items.
2. Share something completed, in progress, and a struggle—Each team member can share items that they have completed since the last meeting. This is often overlooked but should be celebrated. It also provides an opportunity for the team to agree or disagree with the completion of the item. Other team members with different job functions might still have an unfinished task regarding that project, and it is a good way to catch each other. "In Progress" is similar to the three big rocks as described above. A "struggle" provides an excellent opportunity to have team members share a task they are struggling with or stuck on. This provides the team with a chance to assist their colleague and creates a culture of collaboration and cooperation.
3. Allow team discussion items—Most meeting rooms have a whiteboard of some sort. Consider that team members list items on the whiteboard that they would like to discuss as they enter the cabinet meeting. This creates numerous possibilities for the team to engage in problem solving and creates an atmosphere of acceptability for asking others for help and direction.

There are other possible topics and ideas to discuss during a cabinet meeting. One example is leading up to the opening of a new school year. Conversation should center on the status of the numerous tasks required to open the year. The important point is to make the meeting a routine part of your week and to make the discourse flow apparent to participants. They should not spend time wondering what the meeting will be like and what topics might be covered. There is value in the rhythm of communication and an expectation for participation.

As each team member shares, consult your inside sheet for items that pertain to them or any ideas that have a connection. Something a team member shares may connect with an item you have flagged for follow-up under their name on your own sheet. It's also possible a team member's contributions might cause you to list an item to discuss with that person privately during your weekly one-on-one. Your inside sheets also list the topics to cover for the next board meeting (really the next three) as well as workshop topics and educational presentations. Use this time to review responsibilities and make sure all are on the same page. This will set the culture of how your team functions via communication and collaboration.

The final task in a weekly cabinet meeting should be a review of the calendar for the next few weeks. It is important to note who might be on vacation and to assign go-to team members in case of emergencies. It is also a chance to review other important meetings for which the team must prepare together.

Weekly meetings provide opportunities for superintendents to manage the district, the merry-go-round, and the spin of daily life in a large organization. *It is the management of the routine that enables a manager to evolve into a leader.* These meetings are critical for a number of reasons.

- You can give up everything except final responsibility. While you may not be directly involved in the finances or the building and grounds in your district, you are ultimately responsible for them.
- They provide a snapshot of the district. They also provide insight into areas that need attention.
- They provide enough information to prevent surprises. A major rule in most districts is "no surprises." The rhythm of communication is such that your team members can provide you with a "heads-up" on any number of issues.
- They provide a rhythm of communication that beats trying to catch each other between meetings or in the hallways. Communicate with your team to add items to your weekly one-on-one meeting list or hold the item for a cabinet meeting.
- When someone comes to you with an idea, rather than solve that idea right away suggest it be shared at cabinet. A fear all leaders should have is making decisions in isolation or without all possible information. Your suggestion to bring up such items during cabinet meetings will foster a culture of collaboration.
- Weekly meetings establish culture. They emphasize the importance of routine face-to-face meetings, communication, and collaboration.

LET'S GET STARTED!

- Create a routine of weekly one-on-ones.
- Create a routine of weekly cabinet meetings.
- Review the necessary changes in your schedule with your assistant.

Chapter Ten

Weekly Tasks

Beyond the completion of daily tasks, how do you tackle big items like goals and projects? Single tasks are easy and quickly resolved. How do you plan and account for your action steps to complete your goals? What about tackling big projects that may or may not be aligned to your goals? Where do you stop the spin of the merry-go-round and begin? Review the tasks that you completed last week. Do you know how many you completed? Were there a few or many? How did you plan for their completion? Can you point to several completed tasks that moved a goal forward?

These questions center on two words—choice versus chance. Choice is how you determine what you will do because you plan for it, and you make a choice to conduct business a certain way. You make a choice to schedule a weekly review with your assistant once a week and keep the appointment. You make a choice to put on running shoes before sunrise and work out. (Everyone knows workouts don't happen by chance.)

Chance is what most people do. Everyone has goals and projects to complete. Everyone knows what the important big rocks are, and yet, far too often, people don't plan for them. Rarely will happenstance, serendipity, and randomness lead to a successful week or that early morning workout.

There are five days in a week and five days to dedicate to a weekly task or project (the weekends were originally designed for you and nonwork activities). This chapter will present three weekly task routines that you should *choose* to complete. It matters little what day of the week you decide to review your goals or conduct a weekly review. What matters are the choices you make. You decide. The goal is to commit to spending precious time each week in areas of importance to you, your career, and your family.

There are several reasons why you need to make strong choices regarding your weekly tasks.

- Routine—You will find comfort in a system that provides time each week to review and reflect on important goals and projects.
- Consistent focus—Each week you review the status of a goal and commit to at least one action item to advance the goal. Multiply this by the number of goals and projects that are currently on your plate.
- No surprises—Your midyear goal review should never sneak up on you. The project deadline should not alarm you because, each week, you have checked the status, determined the next action step(s), and recorded the task in your system.
- Mountaintop—When your system provides clarity on what is completed and what needs to be completed, there is a sense of being on top of things. You know the feeling when you are in a good space and not playing catch up and leaving things to chance. Athletes call it being in the zone, and it is a wonderful feeling. A system should provide you with a sense of being on top of it all.

Here are three examples of making strong choices in your week. As you review each, think about the flow of your week and what the possibilities are for you to control more of the weekly spin.

GOAL WEDNESDAY

Wednesday is the perfect time to schedule a weekly task to review your progress toward achieving your yearly organizational goals. Call this weekly task, "Goal Wednesday," and use Wednesday's position in the workweek to pause and review what you've accomplished since last Wednesday. It is also time to choose what must happen between now and next Wednesday's review of the goal.

The first step is to create a task that is actually your goal. This step was described in detail in chapter 5. Remember to offset the title with the word "GOAL." Next, immediately brainstorm all the tasks required to move your goal forward to completion by the designated deadline. These tasks are placed in the note field. Once you have thought of all the action steps, reformat them so they appear in order of completion. For now, just list any task you think you might need to complete.

Next, list the start date for the next Wednesday and save. The goal will disappear from your current list and reappear when you arrive at work on Wednesday. This is the beauty and simplicity of pushing tasks and setting them up as reminders on dates you determine. This will create a routine on which you will come to rely. You are now set to revisit this goal and other goals, once a week, on Goal Wednesday.

The objective for this routine is to have at least one action item on your task list each week for each goal. For example, if you have three goals for the year, then each week, you should establish at least one task per goal that you must complete to make progress toward completion. If you don't complete the goal this week, it can carry over and become the next week's task. There will be times when you need to complete more than one task per goal in a given week.

So what really happens on Goal Wednesday? Here is a rundown:

- Your calendar will remind you, during your Daily Setup, that it is Goal Wednesday.
- Dedicate time during the day to review each goal. One option is to schedule thirty minutes each Wednesday for this review and have this as a recurring appointment. You can also review your schedule for the day and select time to review your goals. Your schedule may change, so you will be able to move the thirty-minute chunk of time to an open space as needed.
- Review the past week and ask yourself if you finished the tasks associated with this goal. If so, remove that task from the note field.
- Review your overall status with this goal. Has anything changed since last week?
- Review your list of remaining tasks in the note field. What is the next most logical task required to move the goal forward? Place this in your task list for the coming week.
- Consider what additional tasks might be necessary. Throughout the week, you might decide there are additional components of the goal. Each week provides you with an opportunity to add tasks to your goal, as well as time to check off completed items.
- Continue this review for each goal.
- When your review of all goals is completed, take the final step, and "push" each goal to next Wednesday. You will be ready to repeat the process in one week.

Your goals are too important to leave to chance. Chance is the moment your goal pops into your head and you ask yourself, "What have I done lately to move this goal forward?" This usually happens in the middle of a meeting or during a commute. Goal completion must be a choice. Creating a Goal Wednesday means you are choosing a routine and committing to it one day each week.

TRACKING GOAL PROGRESS

Another critical step in goal completion is the recording of action over the course of the year. Goal Wednesday provides the time to review each goal and also the opportunity to record activities and attach artifacts (agendas, e-mails, and other documents that demonstrate completion of goal-related activities) along the way. Imagine your goal review at the end of the year and your ability to page through numerous examples throughout the year that support your completion of a goal. Part of your goal review should be communicating what you did. The other, equally powerful part, is enhancing the communication of your accomplishment through pages of artifacts.

Consider using a program like Evernote, mentioned in chapter 6, to record your activity. Simply create a note for each goal and include the note as part of your weekly review. As you scan your weekly activity for each goal, list meetings you attended or held related to each goal, as well as the dates. Make sure to include or attach meeting agendas and other supporting documents throughout the year.

PROJECT THURSDAY

What is a project? How does that differ from a task? If you look at your task list, each task should require a single action for completion. For example, return a call. Once it is completed, you can check it off and move to the next task. However, a phone call could be a part of completing a project. You may need to prepare a budget proposal, which could require calling several people to gather information useful in completing the proposal; this is a project.

A project is anything that has more than one step. Review your task list right now and look for items that require multiple steps to complete. Here is where you will find your projects. It is a small and simple distinction. Your daily task list should contain only single-action items. Some projects will have numerous steps and might need the assistance of project management software. Other projects might only take three or four steps for completion.

Why Thursdays? No reason here other than it is another day of the week. It can easily be moved and called Project Tuesday. The important thing is to decide on a day, and stick with it. Project Thursday (or Tuesday) should become part of the routine and choices you make each week.

The first step toward implementing Project Thursday is to create a task and project title, described in chapter 5. Remember to offset the title with the word "PROJECT." Next, immediately brainstorm all the tasks needed to move forward with your project. These tasks are placed in the note field. Once you have thought of all the action steps, reformat them to be in order of completion. For now, just list any task you think you might need to complete.

Next, list the start date for the next Thursday and save. The project will disappear from your current list and reappear when you arrive at work next Thursday. You are now set to revisit this project and other projects once a week.

Follow the same pattern for your projects as you do for Goal Wednesday. Remember to track your progress in a document or note-taking system such as Evernote. Again, the point is to create at least one task each week that is required to move the project forward.

POSITIVE NOTES

There is nothing that replaces the power of a handwritten note. While there may be opportunities during the week to think of jotting a quick "Thank You" or "Good Job" note, choose to commit to this task once a week.

Simply create a recurring task, as described in chapter 5, with the title "Write a Positive Note." Create it as a high priority task (must be done today), and think of at least one person who you should thank or praise. Once in the habit of doing this, perhaps every Tuesday, you will undoubtedly find yourself writing several notes each Tuesday.

The return on a few minutes of your time each week is tremendous. Employees will appreciate your recognition and often save the notes. It is a little thing that you should make a choice to do and schedule it once a week. Do not forget your family; a quick note to your spouse, significant other, or child in college is equally important.

Again, review your list of tasks and your unique work environment for other similar opportunities to let routines remove some of the load from your mind. As you begin to implement the ideas in this book, allow yourself to be creative and change the rules and stretch your thinking.

This really comes down to the battle for your attention, or what might be called "attention management." There are articles available that discuss how to better manage your attention in a world of social media and a seemingly faster spinning merry-go-round. Goals and projects are important and do not complete themselves. Make a choice to benefit from a routine that will return once a week during your Daily Setup. It is a game changer for your week!

LET'S GET STARTED!

- Pick one goal and brainstorm action steps in the note field.
- Add one action step to your task list and push the goal forward to the day of the week you select.
- Repeat for your remaining goals.
- Pick one project and brainstorm action steps.

- Add one action step to your task list and push the project forward to the day of the week you select.
- Set up a weekly recurring task to write at least one positive note.

Part Three

Monthly Routines

In part 3, we explore routines that can maximize your effectiveness by month. There are monthly board meetings and meetings with others on your team or employee groups that require routine and consistent attention. One of the most important monthly meetings is with you and is called "Leadership Lunch with Me." Once a month, take time to reflect on you and how effectively you are managing your plate. Many of the meetings you attend and are responsible for have accompanying tasks that need to be completed on a monthly basis, which is the focus of chapter 10. Chapter 11 presents an activity to create a list, by month, of the various tasks that are due either on a monthly basis or during certain months. This list will become a part of your weekly review.

Chapter Eleven

Monthly Meetings

Take a look at your month at-a-glance calendar and identify the monthly meetings that happen each month. There are certainly administrative team meetings, employee group meetings, or board meetings. Consider the meetings that you are responsible for as opposed to community boards on which you serve. What system do you use to prepare for these meetings?

There is a routine to these meetings and they provide touch points with members of your team. For your board of directors, there are planning and action meetings and perhaps committee meetings each month. These are public performances that you are responsible for leading, and they require planning that happens by choice, not chance.

How often do you meet with your leadership team? The decision is yours, and what you do speaks volumes about the culture and climate of your organization. Where do you hold your team meetings? Again, this choice illustrates the workplace environment you create and are responsible for cultivating. Do your team members dread the meetings or would they like to have more? Most importantly, have you asked them? There can be no substitute for face-to-face time between you and your team. E-mails and phone calls pale in comparison to meetings where everyone is in the room.

MONTHLY MEETINGS

There are several different types of meetings that can be held monthly or during certain months. For the purposes of this chapter, consider first a meeting with yourself, then team meetings, board meetings, and subsets of those mentioned above.

LEADERSHIP LUNCH WITH ME

Your calendar should contain one recurring appointment—with yourself. This appointment, called "Leadership Lunch with Me," is time to review, reflect, and plan. You'll need a journal-type notebook, pen, and list of questions before you arrive. The goal is to review your successes, challenges, and personal and professional status since your last lunch.

• Review—What has happened since your last leadership lunch with you? Did you keep the promises you made? Did you tackle the stretch goal you thought was a good idea last month?
• Reflect—What was the last month like for you as a leader? When the organization was counting on you, how did you perform? Being the leader is often overrated and few know the burdens placed on superintendents. How are you doing? Physically? Mentally? How is your family?
• Plan—So, based on the above, what do you want to do now? What area is in need of immediate attention? What area are you avoiding? What conversation needs to take place

How a Leadership Lunch with Me Could Work for You

• Pack your bag: Before you leave the office, make sure you have a notebook, pen, and list of questions. (See the starter list of questions included below.) Go to a bookstore and select a nice, hardcover notebook that you are comfortable with and select a nice pen that you will look forward to using each month. This is a way to treat yourself and, often, the little things matter.
• Pick a spot: Find a nice "sit-down" restaurant and order something a little more expensive than normal. Once a month, you are worth it! Make sure you have a table for four so you can stretch out and have plenty of writing space. If possible, ask to sit in the back of the restaurant or a corner with a window for natural light. You will find favorite restaurants and favorite spots in each.
• Reflect: After you order, take a moment to review your questions and the previous months' answers. Start reviewing your questions for this month, one-by-one. Take a moment to think deeply and answer honestly.
• Write: Record your reflections in your notebook so you can review, at your next lunch with yourself, to see what has changed or where you have grown. You can also use a technology tool such as Evernote to capture your thoughts.

You might be thinking you don't have time for this meeting. But how can you not find time, once a month, to meet with yourself? Most folks think superintendents are pretty busy. A typical request for a meeting usually begins with, "I know you are really busy, but. . . ." The truth is—not so. Take a look at the typical principal or teacher day and, there, you will find busy. As a superintendent, you are more in control of your schedule than others.

To make the most of your lunch, develop questions in advance to help focus your time. The goal is a sustained, big picture conversation that carries over to the next month. Here are some sample questions for your lunch:

- What challenges can I learn from?
- What successes can I learn from?
- What do I need to do, learn, or read to become a better leader?
- What is the most important decision I am facing? What is keeping me from making it?
- How would I like to be different next month?
- How am I different from my last lunch?
- What would I say to me, if I were sitting across the table from myself?

The first couple of meetings might feel somewhat awkward. There is a disconnect with having lunch by yourself for sixty to ninety minutes when society tells you to keep running. There is always so much to do! Don't despair! Keep holding the meeting and you will soon come to rely on the chance to check in with yourself.

Imagine sitting down to review several years' worth of journals that chronicle your experiences as a superintendent. For those of you looking to write a book, this is excellent material. For those of you serious about mentoring new superintendents, your experiences throughout the years can help others along their journeys.

LEADERSHIP TEAM MEETINGS

The frequency of meetings with members of your leadership team depends on your organization's size and situation. The importance, however, cannot be underestimated. Team meetings are critical to make sure all things run smoothly.

The location for meetings can vary according to your preference. There are certainly times to hold meetings in the central office, away from distractions in school buildings. Here, central office staff members are accessible and should be a part of the agenda. The need to constantly calibrate efficiencies among the business office, the transportation office, and the special education department is essential.

Consider holding team meetings in various buildings throughout the school year. This establishes a presence for your team and visibility for central office staff and those from other buildings. There is real power in having central office team members join in classroom walk throughs and see the inside of classrooms. The hosting principal creates teams of two to three administrators that visit a designated classroom. Sometimes, there might be a focus for the walkthrough, such as a district initiative. Other times, it might be to have high school administrators see a kindergarten classroom and elementary principals to experience a high school classroom.

Depending on the size of your district, it might be optimal for you to hold elementary and secondary principal meetings each month. The superintendent, assistant superintendent(s), or the principals themselves can lead these. If collaboration is a part of your culture, these meetings need to be a part of your organizational fabric.

It is a good idea each summer to review last year's monthly meetings and make plans to change where necessary. It is also a good idea to schedule the meeting dates each month prior to the start of the school year. Once the year starts, calendars fill with numerous meetings. Schedule these meetings with your team in advance and communicate your expectations for attendance.

EMPLOYEE GROUPS

Does your calendar contain routine meetings with the various employee groups in your organization? Your communication approach is just as important with employee groups as it is with your cabinet or team. Consider establishing routine meetings with the following groups:

- Teachers' association—Schedule a monthly opportunity to talk with the leadership of the teachers' association. It should be a routine that provides a chance for ideas to be exchanged and a chance to evaluate the status of your relationship.
- Support staff—The support staff members are vital to the overall functionality of the school district. Do you know how they feel about their jobs and the district? What might you be missing if you don't have an ongoing conversation with this group?

One warning—never let a burning issue wait until the next scheduled meeting. While routine is nice, it should never substitute for a pressing issue. Create a rule that if there is a pressing issue, the meeting is today. Consider the other groups in your district and ask yourself whether there is benefit to scheduling routine meetings. There can also be quarterly scheduled meetings for certain groups.

BOARD MEETINGS

Depending on your circumstance, you may have one board meeting a month or more. There are also committee meetings and requirements such as negotiations meetings. Clearly, these meetings are important and have many moving parts. It is critical to your success to have a routine each month.

Do you know which routine items will appear before the board in the next three months? Where do you record items that happen during the month that you might want to include on a future board meeting agenda? How do you plan for board workshops and executive sessions and where do you record it all?

Several times throughout this book the "inside sheets" are mentioned. Here is another great example of using the sheets to always know—at least three months into the future—which items will come before the board. Here is how it works:

- Dates—Across the top list the meeting dates for the next three months of board meetings. If you ever need to know when the next meeting is scheduled within the next three months, a quick look at your inside sheet will suffice.
- Workshops—What topics are scheduled for a workshop for the board? List the items here and review with your cabinet and other members of your team that might need to be involved. In the next chapter, an activity to create a yearly board workshop calendar will be shared.
- Administrative report—Once a month, various administrators might provide an update to the board. List the items you plan to share with the board in this space.
- Discussion items—Here are the routine and nonroutine items for you to record each month. Continue to delete past months and add new months and nothing should sneak up on you.
- Executive session—You never know when or where you will be when an item pops up that you need to discuss with the board in executive session. Simply open your inside sheet and record.
- Educational focus presentation—Perhaps you have a presentation once a month that focuses on an educational topic. You can record the topic here.
- Agenda items—This small space is for any last-minute items that appear between your planning and action meetings (if your district has two). While most items are discussed in public during the planning meeting, sometimes there are last-minute additions to the agenda and you can list them here.
- Superintendent's announcements—Once a month, you might share various announcements with the board. Record those topics here.

As mentioned in chapter 9, weekly cabinet meetings are a perfect time to review the upcoming board meetings. Do you have a routine for when agenda items are due? Does everyone on the team know this deadline? How do you handle last-minute items? Use your cabinet meetings as a way to plan for agenda creation and publication. Consider holding cabinet meetings the morning after each board meeting to debrief.

Another excellent trick is to always print a paper copy of the board agenda and work from that copy throughout the meeting. While it is good to convert your board meetings to a paperless solution, sometimes technology fails. If so, you will always have a hard copy and can move forward.

The other reason for a printed copy is the two-pen method. During the meeting, take notes in either a black or blue pen. When an item comes up that you need to take some action on in the future, record it with a red pen. It does not matter who is responsible for the actual task. If the administration needs to follow up on an item, write it in red. Tomorrow morning, during your cabinet meeting, you will determine who will complete the task and when it will be completed. Thus, your agenda should be a mix of two colored pens that contain notes and tasks.

BOARD LEADERSHIP MEETINGS

Board leadership meetings are held on a monthly basis following the one or two normal board meetings. Membership in the meeting can be simply you and the board president. It may also include the other officers your board determines as appropriate.

This meeting provides an excellent opportunity to review the current month's meetings, future meetings, and the board's calendar of events.

- Items from this month—What items from this month's meetings need to be carried over to next month's meetings? Does the board need to follow up on items? For example, if your board decides to write a letter to local legislators in support of a proposed education bill, who will draft it and provide to the board to review and edit?
- Items for next month's agenda—What are the routine items that normally appear this month? What items need to be carried over each month? This meeting is also a time to talk about logistics and overall functioning of board meetings. How can you help the board run more effective and efficient meetings?
- Future calendar items—What workshops are scheduled over the next few months? What educational topics or initiatives would the board like to learn more about through a public presentation during a future meeting?

MEETING MANAGEMENT

How do you currently plan for your monthly meetings? Who is responsible for agenda creation and completion? At what point prior to the meeting do you publish the agenda? If you are like most superintendents, you manage and lead numerous meetings each month.

In chapter 6, inside sheets were reviewed as a means to record any number of thoughts for yourself and for others. Another wonderful use of the inside sheets is to manage the numerous meetings you lead. As you travel throughout your day, your inside sheet will be the go-to place to record ideas for future meetings. If you are at your desk, you certainly can build the agenda in a document or list the ideas in the note field of the meeting appointment, as explained earlier. Edit the form to meet your meeting needs and be prepared to list any meeting agenda ideas, no matter your location.

So what are the meetings that you have on a monthly basis? What are the routine touch points that are important to you? There is a routine to everyone's month and you must examine yours and plan accordingly. Choose today to take control of your monthly meetings.

LET'S GET STARTED!

- Conduct a review of the last twelve months and look for routine meetings.
- Determine the employee groups you should be meeting with on a monthly basis.
- Schedule leadership lunches with me for the next twelve months and gather the necessary supplies.
- Conduct a conversation with your board about monthly meetings and discuss ways to improve organization and communication.
- Create an inside sheet for meeting management and make its use a routine part of your system.

Chapter Twelve

Monthly Tasks

If you step back and reflect on the past several months, not only will you notice the emergence of patterns and trends within your schedule, but, among these, you will also find tasks that occur monthly. As you review your previous schedules and tasks, write down the tasks for which you are responsible. While a board meeting is an event in your schedule, there are numerous tasks that must be completed and need a school leader's attention each month. This repetition is another example of the routine of tasks on a monthly basis.

August happens once a year. It should never sneak up on you. The start of the school year, usually in August, is not a mystery. Are you prepared for it when it comes? When does your preparation for the school year begin? As mentioned above, create a list of all the tasks that you are responsible for to open the school year.

There are two types of monthly tasks that you must handle. The first type is a once-a-month task. Preparations for a board meeting and completing your monthly expense report are once-a-month tasks. The second type of tasks refers to those which only must be completed during certain months in the year. Examples of these tasks include staff orientation at the start of a new school year and the creation of a school calendar for the upcoming year.

ONCE-A-MONTH TASKS

Board Meetings

Board meetings are a major responsibility of superintendents. There are numerous moving parts to pulling off one or more public meetings each month. Consider the following:

- How is the agenda created? This routine event and its accompanying tasks should not be left to chance. You must determine when the agenda needs to be finalized and posted.
- Agenda items—There are many departments that contribute to the agenda each month. Does everyone on your team know when and how to submit items each month? Examples include personnel items, education items, financial items, and more. You must also remember to include all the supporting documentation for each agenda item as well.
- Presentations—Will there be an educational focus presentation each month that will require students, teachers, and parents to be in attendance at a board meeting? When will those decisions be made and communicated? Who will handle the logistics?
- Workshops—Is there a scheduled workshop for the board on a specific topic? Who is responsible for the materials and presentations?
- Executive sessions—When do you communicate the need to hold an executive session and who is responsible for its preparation? If it is a legal or real estate item, you should include your business manager and solicitor. If it is a personnel item, remember to include your director of human resources if appropriate.
- Communications—How do you communicate your board meetings to the public each month? Consider various avenues to publicize your meetings and plan for this as a routine, monthly task.

There are certainly other considerations that are unique to each school district. No two districts run meetings, committee meetings, or community meetings in the same fashion. The key is to treat these recurring calendar items as recurring tasks. If there is a deadline for all agenda items on the first day of each month, add a reminder task on the twenty-fifth day of each month. Board meetings are too important to leave to chance. Commit to the monthly tasks necessary for successful monthly meetings.

Alpha Files

Chapter 3 provided you with an overview of a filing system using Alpha Files. They are a great way to keep items from sitting on top of tables and your desk. However, if all you do is place items in there each month, the files will fill up over time. One technique to avoid this is to create a monthly task to review and purge. Create a recurring monthly task labeled "Review Alpha Files" and set it for the fifteenth day of each month (or whatever day makes sense to you).

During your Daily Setup on the fifteenth of each month, you will see the task reappear and remind you to review and clean out the file. This is important, and will keep the files from growing to a size where they become unmanageable. It is also somewhat of a safety valve. You will find comfort in knowing that, at least once each month, you will review each file. There are times when you will find certain items that were placed here temporarily and forgotten.

The routine is pretty simple. Start with the letter "A" and pull all items onto your desktop. Review each item and determine if there is some action that needs to occur. You might discard an item that is no longer needed. You might also return items to the same Alpha File. Perhaps you created a file with other material that came across your desk in the last month, and now want to relocate this information to a new file. This simple file review takes about fifteen minutes and will remind you of your filed items and their locations at least once each month.

Leadership Lunch with Me

In chapter 11, leadership lunch with me was presented as an excellent way to spend quality time with yourself to review, reflect, and plan. The scheduling of this lunch appointment should be a recurring task each month that can be handled in one of two ways:

1. Create a recurring task each month on a date you specify. When the item appears in your task list during your Daily Setup, you can quickly look at your calendar. When you find an appropriate time slot, simply enter the appointment with yourself, and then check the task "complete."
2. Create a recurring task once a year. If you use July 15, during your Daily Setup you will be reminded of the need to schedule these lunches each month. This will require a little more time to schedule each month, but will place this important item well in advance for the coming year. You can always change the actual date if necessary, but the task can be completed once a year as well.

Leadership Team Meetings

Whatever the frequency or type of team meetings held each month, they require equal attention and preparation. There are several considerations, including the following:

- Scheduling—Do you sit as a team and create your meetings for the year?
- Location—Where do you hold meetings with your team? There are times to pull principals out of their buildings to avoid distractions. There are also times to visit buildings as a team. A team meeting held in a building also

provides opportunities for administrators to conduct walkthroughs in classrooms.

- Attendees—Who should attend certain meetings and who should remain behind to cover a building? It is certainly beneficial to have all members on the team in attendance, but having a presence in a building is also important.
- Agenda—How do you build the agenda each month? There are probably standing items that need to be reviewed, such as department updates (building and grounds, food service, business office, transportation). Prior to the meeting, ask your team for agenda items that are timely and need discussion. Determine the appropriate lead-time for you. Two weeks prior to the meeting enables you to create the agenda and publish a week prior to the meeting. This is an opportunity to create a recurring task on a monthly basis.

Family and Personal Items

As you build a system of routines in one place, it must account for who you are outside of work. While this system will improve your efficiency and effectiveness during your work day, it should also improve your ability to be a better spouse, significant other, parent, brother or sister, son or daughter, volunteer, scrap booker, and stamp collector.

If you review your schedule and tasks over the last month, where would any of the personal areas listed above come into play? How can you use the tools provided in this book to maximize your time both in and out of work? Here are several suggestions:

- Anniversary—While the big date might only be once a year, consider this special date as an opportunity to express your affection and appreciation. If the date is February 24, place a task to purchase something special one month prior to the date. This date should never sneak up on you!
- Parents—The life and hours of a superintendent can become overwhelming and demanding of your time. The evening commitments are frequent, and we all know that is part of the job. If you are blessed to have both parents still with you and they are local, schedule lunch or dinner appointments with them before evening meetings.
- Children—How will you balance the demands of the job and the demands of raising a family? What special dates and appointments need to be placed in your calendar and task list?

A final piece of advice—if you are the superintendent, you get to decide the work and life balance of those under your care. There is no valor in working too many hours, and thus requiring others to maintain the same schedule. Life is short. Children grow up way too fast. Parents don't live forever. You are in a unique position to matter in the lives of every single member of your team. Do you require them to attend unnecessary meetings? Do you require too many nights out? If you model the need to be everywhere and at every meeting, what do you think will become the norm on your team? If you model a balanced approach, this will become the culture on your team. Don't forget that you matter.

CERTAIN MONTH TASKS

As stated before, August should not sneak up on you. The start of the school year is an event that requires many tasks. The same holds true for any number of tasks throughout the school year. Even if it only needs attention once or a few times per year, chance is not a strategy. Here are some examples:

- Beginning or end of the school year—As the person responsible for everything, are you ready to open the school year? This is a question that should begin long before the current year ends. The personnel process and the filling of staff vacancies include tasks that require your oversight. Do you need to prepare opening remarks or closing remarks? If you have not done so, take a few moments right now and brainstorm all the tasks associated with the beginning and end of the school year and enter them into your system. Some tasks might be a single action task, and others might be more in line with a project that contains multiple steps. Refer back to chapter 5 for descriptions of each.
- Budget calendar—Each year, the budget process has a beginning, middle, and end. What month does the process start for members on your team? If it is November, place a task several months prior to plan the budget calendar and deadlines. This process should never sneak up on you, either!
- Student picture day—Here is a wonderful example for principals. Student picture day happens once a year and there are forms for parents to complete and scheduling needs for the day. Planning for this day should begin months in advance.

What are other examples that come to mind? Whether the task is an every-month task or a certain-month task, others will look to you to plan appropriately. If you model this level of organization, chances are others will, too. One key activity that will help you manage all of this is to develop a monthly task list.

MONTHLY TASK LIST

Ask yourself to list the broad areas which you are responsible for and begin to make a list based on these. Here are three: your office, school board, and the district.

- Your office—What monthly routine items originate from your office each month? How about certain months over the course of a year? This is the easiest place to start.
- School board—What monthly items are necessary to keep the board functioning? There are usually agenda items each month for approval, as well as preparation for retreats and conferences.
- The district—What items need your attention from the macro level? There are opening and closing ceremonies and retirement recognition tasks that must be handled.

There are two ways to conduct an exercise to create your monthly task list, and the way you choose likely depends on whether you are reading this book in your first year as a superintendent or after the completion of several years. If this is your first year, consider creating your list as part of your weekly review. Each week with your assistant, review the tasks that you completed and ask yourself if they are once-a-month tasks or certain-month tasks. Begin to add tasks to the corresponding monthly list and continue each week throughout the year.

If you have completed a year or more, consider the following:

- Secure a boardroom or large office that provides plenty of space.
- Hang twelve sheets of large butcher-block paper on the walls of the room. You can also use twelve sheets of regular 8" x 11" paper around a large table. If you are conducting this exercise with others, it is a good idea to use large paper so that your team reviews the year as they move around the room. Label each page with the month in large letters at the top.
- Bring your calendar from last year, if applicable. Also, secure the last twelve months of board meeting agendas to review. It might be helpful to have two to three years' worth of agendas to determine if action items always or usually occur during a certain month. Prior to the session, brainstorm with your assistant any other schedules that might be of value for the exercise. Don't worry about trying to be too comprehensive. A good system will allow you to review these lists routinely and add items throughout the year.
- Start with the current month or begin from the start of the year. Review what you did in August to prepare for the opening of school. Begin to list these items on the "August" sheet of paper. Move to September and con-

tinue throughout the year. Often, a task in October will jog your memory of a task in August, and you can simply move to that piece of paper and add it there.

If this is your first year, you can conduct this exercise in a similar fashion with your assistant and, perhaps, a key member of your cabinet. Your assistant can bring along his or her calendar or your predecessor's to review. While you may choose to deviate somewhat from your predecessor, it is wise to consider the items from his or her list as well.

When you are finished, review the year and consider the big picture view. Also, consider sharing this list with the board if they do not have a current list of agenda items by month. When completed, type the list into a document for reference during your weekly review.

Again, August should never sneak up on you. A monthly task list is critical to managing the routines of your office, the board, and the district. There is much riding on your organizational ability and many depend on you, both in the office and at home. This is a simple activity that will take no more than an hour or two to complete. The list also fits in nicely with your overall system that begins with a Daily Setup each day and ends the week with a weekly review. The weekly review provides for a continual three-month projection into your future. Now, the only area left to discuss is an opportunity to look at your world from a yearly perspective.

LET'S GET STARTED!

- Set aside time to conduct the activity to create your monthly task list.
- Determine tasks that occur each month.
- Determine tasks that occur during certain months.
- Publish your monthly task list and review with your board and team.

Part Four

Yearly Routine

In part 4, a yearly routine is presented that enables you to finish a school year and turn the corner to approach a new year. This activity requires a review of last year that includes your schedule, workload, successes and failures, and your monthly leadership lunches with you. There is value in an offsite review of your year that involves goal-setting for the coming year. You will ask yourself, "One year from now, what is it that I want to do or become?" You have an appointment with yourself in one year. What changes are necessary in your daily, weekly, and monthly routines to become the human being you are capable of and to fulfill your hopes and dreams?

Chapter Thirteen

Year in Review

WHAT IS IT?

The year in review is a wonderful opportunity for you to step back from the everyday flow of your world and reflect on who you are as a professional and as a person. While there are daily, weekly, and monthly appointments and tasks, this is special because it happens just once a year. It is also special, because it involves traveling to a location away from your office and home. This type of big-picture thinking should take place somewhere you can break away from the usual routine. For some, it might be the beach or the mountains. For others, it could be a quiet place, like a college library or park.

The purpose of this yearly review is to survey where you are in your career and your personal life. You are complex and unique, as are your goals, relationships, and aspirations and the year in review provides time to focus on *all* of these and most importantly—*you*.

REFLECT AND PROJECT

The purpose of reflecting on the past year is to learn from it. This time has passed and will not return, yet the past contains lessons from which you can learn and use to craft your future personal and professional goals. The saying "it is what it is" might be true about last year, but reflecting on "what was" is your opportunity to plan for "what could be" in the next year. The operative question is this—one year from now, what is it I would like to accomplish, be, do, or experience? How can you make today better than yesterday, this week better than the last week, and this year better than last year?

A large or ambitious goal may take several years to complete. Break your goal into one-year increments. What items on your list would you like to accomplish professionally and personally and when? Consider your work team, your family, areas for your personal growth, and opportunities for you to contribute to the development of others. Imagine what you want to be and how you want to feel exactly one year from now when you conduct this exercise again. Write these thoughts in a journal and you will be ahead of most others. Translate these thoughts, hopes, and dreams into next action steps and begin. Remember that you have this appointment in one year, so don't let yourself down.

WHERE AND WHEN?

The location of your year in review is up to you. What place holds special significance for you? It could be the beach or a lakeside cabin. If you are a big city person, find a place there suitable for this type of exercise. If you are new to the year in review, consider any place that is not a normal destination for you on a daily basis. The importance of the location is that it signals to your brain the significance of this activity. It should not be rushed in between weekends throughout the year. This is a special time and the sole focus is on you. Again, initially the activity might feel awkward. However, as you conduct these reviews, you will come to enjoy the opportunity to take stock of your station in this world and the significance of your position. Others are counting on you professionally and personally.

While the summer provides a natural break from the school year and a chance for renewal, it is not the only time you can conduct your year in review. New Year's Day, for example, is an opportune time to reflect and project. There may be other trips you take during the year when you can conduct your year in review. Also, consider New Year's Day as a midyear check to see how your promises have withstood half a year. If you are doing well, treat yourself. If you have not made progress, consider that you still have another half of a year (until that summer meeting with yourself) to deliver on your hopes and dreams.

PROCESS

There are several ways to conduct the year in review. There were goals from last year, as well as relationships, to think about. Also, consider how your schedule impacts your ability to manage and lead. Which tasks did you struggle with? Which projects from last year offer lessons from which you can learn? Consider the areas listed below when developing your own year in review:

- Professional—Overall, how was your year? What were the high points and the low points? There is power in reflecting on all the good and the not-so-good events. Ask yourself, how much of it did you control? How much was your doing or your fault? Bring your calendar and scroll, week by week, to review your activities. You will be amazed how much you forgot about last October.
- Personal—What lessons can you learn from events that happened with your family or friends? How is your health? Are you raising children and, if so, what were the high points and low points to take away from the year? On the other side of children, how are your parents doing? What kind of support can you provide them as they age? Again, a calendar review should help here, provided you record family appointments in the same place as work appointments.
- Goals—What were yours from last year? Do you want to write a book? Open a business or investigate creating a limited liability corporation (LLC)? If you conduct yearly reviews, you should have a few goals from last summer. If not, begin listing them now.
- Relationships—What are the professional and personal relationships that matter to you? Write them down and spend some time to review the status of each one. Ask yourself, have they grown, remained stagnant, or regressed over the last year? This tough conversation with yourself will set the stage for determining what attention you will pay in the coming year to these relationships.
- Leadership Lunches with Me—In chapter 11, leadership lunch with me was presented as a means to spend some time, monthly, with just you to consider the areas mentioned above. The year in review provides an excellent time to review your journal notes from each month.
- Calendar—As you review each month, reflect on the amount of appointments and what was within your control. Were there too many? Too few? What was the frequency of team meetings over the past year? When did it feel as if there were the right amount of appointments and time to complete tasks? This is a great opportunity to make some notes, return to the office, and have a great conversation with your assistant.
- Projects and tasks—Review your monthly lists to find items to add and remove from your monthly lists. Ask yourself what projects or tasks provided a challenge and perhaps need more lead-time. Where did you delegate well and where can you improve? It is also a good time to review the major responsibilities of those on your team.

Consider using a journal, perhaps the one you use for your monthly leadership lunches, to take notes as you work through the areas listed above. Consider other areas that make sense to you and help you to improve. Remember to project out one, two, or five years and commit to growth. Spending time each summer, or when you take your vacation, is making a clear choice and leaving nothing to chance. And if you don't take a vacation or time off, start now.

A final comment about "working" on vacation . . . the year in review is more than work. It is a dedication to you and all your various responsibilities. Taking time to reflect on your status is a wonderful habit to model for those at work, as well as those at home. You decide exactly when it happens on vacation, but there is nothing wrong with your kids seeing a parent think and plan.

LET'S GET STARTED!

- Determine the date and location to conduct your first year in review.
- Gather necessary materials for the experience.
- Have a conversation with your assistant prior to and after your review.
- Share with your team, both in the office and on the home front, the purpose of your year in review.
- Share with your family and encourage them to complete a year in review as well.

Chapter Fourteen

In Closing

So there you have it—daily, weekly, monthly, and yearly routines to help you manage and lead. If you have made it this far, you are experiencing improved clarity about what you need to and should accomplish each day. You are also spending time each week reviewing your goals, reviewing your projects, reviewing your schedule three weeks into the future, and reviewing responsibilities for the coming three months. While you may have found it awkward, you are taking yourself out to lunch once a month and reviewing your monthly task lists. And while you may not have arrived at your year in review, the thought of what types of promises you will make to yourself for next year are already forming.

Perhaps you experienced a fusion of ideas from this book and the organization of your office that provided an improved sense of what needs to be accomplished in your journey at work and at home. You may have also shared some ideas with others and created a small group of folks who like to work at being better organized each day. It is okay; there are similar groups of like-minded people out there.

Here are some big ideas from the book to review.

ROUTINES

As much as possible, consider what decisions and actions you can make as routine as possible. We all become fatigued at some point in the day with the numerous questions and decisions coming our direction. Consider small decisions that you must make before you come to work each day, like what to wear or what to eat for breakfast. Ask your assistant to provide a perspective of his or her own and you might be amazed at the possibilities.

The goal is really to simplify your day as much as possible so you can focus on the big rocks. You know, the goals and projects that you review mentally on your drive home and kick yourself for not making much progress on that day. Remember, you are the leader and everyone is counting on you to keep the big rocks moving. There are no prizes for the most minor decision made in a day. Be done with the minutiae and focus on important work.

How can you determine what can be accomplished on "autopilot" so that your brain is free to really think about the vision and future of your organization? Let's start with what to wear each day and breakfast, and continue to the daily recording of tasks and creating a filing system where everything has a place and your workspace is clear. The goal is to arrive where your weekly meetings enable those who need some personal time with you to have some personal time with you and eliminate needless interruptions throughout each day.

ONE LIST

You are simply one person. Each person needs one list, whether you have a full-time job during the day and one or more in the evening. Oh, and don't forget scouts, church, and volunteer boards. Why would you ever create numerous calendars and lists to keep it all together? You can only be in one place at a time and can only mentally process one thing at a time. Find a calendar and task list that works for you and make that your total solution.

RECORD EVERYTHING

Every time a thought or idea pops into your head, find a system that enables you to record it immediately before it leaves your short-term memory. How many times has this happened to you: You are driving and using this time to review your ideas, projects, and goals and something brilliant pops into your head . . . only to be completely forgotten a few minutes later? Yes, it might come back to your short-term memory, but it might not, or not in time.

Whether you use a tablet and pen in the car or some technology or app on your smartphone, record your thoughts or send e-mails to yourself immediately so you won't lose them. It is acceptable to stop the treadmill to make a note of something, regardless of what the person next to you thinks. The goal is to capture all the thoughts or ideas throughout your day because you never know when something magnificent will hit.

ELIMINATE THE URGENT

As much as possible, your goal is to be prepared for what is next on your schedule and the big meeting next week or next month. Board meetings and administrative team meetings rarely sneak up on anyone. They are right there on your schedule a few weeks from now. Implement the ideas and steps in this book to reduce the urgency of the known and you will find you are better able to prioritize and act when the urgency of the unknown pops up.

BE HUMAN

Realize you are only human and that everyone fails to execute from time to time. Regardless of who you are, there are times when we just fail to plan. Recommit to your system and climb back to the top of the pile. Let others on your team in on your journey to be better organized, and share when times are tough and when times are good. We all fight the battle each day with twenty-four hours; my wish is that you win more than you lose.

LET'S GET STARTED!

- Keep a journal of the ideas that worked and why.
- Share two ideas from this book with others on your team.
- Improve upon the ideas in this book! I would love to hear from you regarding improvements and suggestions.

Appendix

A.1—MEETING NOTES FORM

Meeting Title: _____ **Date:** _____

| Start Time: | Present: |
| End Time: | Absent: |

!	Action Items	Responsible	Due Date

!	Communication Tasks?	Responsible	Due Date

	Meeting Notes

Meeting Notes

A.2—INSIDE SHEET—CABINET/BOARD/MEETING MANAGEMENT

CABINET		
Asst. Superintendent	**Technology/Transportation**	**Business Manager**
Director of IT	**Director of Communications**	**Director Human Resources**
Asst. Business Manager	**Building & Grounds**	**Facility Director**

BOARD		
Board Update	**Board President**	**Board Leadership Mtg.**
		Board Workshop Ideas
Solicitor		

MEETING MANAGEMENT		
Leadership Team	**Elementary**	**Secondary**
Cabinet Meeting	**Misc.**	**Policy Advisory**

A.3—INSIDE SHEET—ROLLING THREE-MONTH BOARD MEETING MANAGEMENT

Board Agenda Items		
January 6 **Planning Meeting** Workshop	**February 3** **Planning Meeting** Workshop	**March 10** **Planning Meeting** Workshop
Administrative Report	Administrative Report	Administrative Report
Discussion Items	Discussion Items	Discussion Items
Executive Session	Executive Session	Executive Session
January 13 **Action Meeting** Workshop	**February 10** **Action Meeting** Workshop	**March 17** **Action Meeting** Workshop
Ed Focus Presentation	Ed Focus Presentation	Ed Focus Presentation
Agenda Items	Agenda Items	Agenda Items
Superintendent's Announcements	Superintendent's Announcements	Superintendent's Announcements
Executive Session	Executive Session	Executive Session

About the Author

Michael S. Snell, EdD, is superintendent of Central York School District, a K–12 public school district serving 5,700 students in grades K–12. He has held the position since 2009.

Dr. Snell received his Doctor of Education in educational administration from Temple University and his Master of Education in educational leadership and policy studies from the same university. He received his Bachelor of Science degree in secondary education/social studies from Kutztown University. Dr. Snell is a member of the American Association of School Administrators, the National Council of Educational Research and Technology, and the Urban Superintendent's Association of America. Dr. Snell joined Central York School District as assistant superintendent in 2007. Prior to that time, Dr. Snell served as assistant superintendent of West York Area School District from 2003 through 2007; principal of West York Area Middle School from 1998 to 2003; and assistant principal in the Hempfield School District from 1994 to 1998. He taught social studies and civics locally from 1989 to 1994.

In addition to his professional affiliations, Dr. Snell is involved in several community activities throughout York County. He serves on the board of directors of the York County Economic Alliance and the advisory board of the Byrnes Health Education Center.

Dr. Snell consults with school leaders and teams interested in improving organization and leadership and has presented on this topic regionally.

Professional | Personal

- teachers
  staff
- Asst. Prin.
- Diversity Comm.
- discipline
- visiting classroom
- students
  - learning
    relationships

- Family
  (4 kids)
- Laundry
- clean house
- friends
- schedules

- doctoral program
- professional development

- family dinner
- play dates
- family visity events